JP has made diverse professional, academic, & personal contributions in the international arena, including import/export of agricultural machinery, computer hardware, & food perishables; multinationals' business development, brand & financial management, operations analysis, & team leadership; & teaching undergraduate and graduate international business, economics, and statistics.

JP loves cooking and tasting foods of all sorts and origins; exploring his home state of Texas, his home country of Costa Rica, and the rest of the world with his wife Laura and two daughters Emma and Stella; and can often be found in his "happy place" watching a Costa Rica, Brazil, or a USA national soccer team match.

Zoe So

Zoe joined Whole Planet Foundation in June 2016 as a Program Manager supporting the Africa and Middle East portfolio and is currently the Regional Director for the East & South Africa Region.

Prior to joining WPF, Zoe started an independent consultancy specializing in program strategies and partnership development for NGOs and social enterprises. She worked at BRAC USA for three years, where she supported financial inclusion and youth empowerment initiatives in Uganda, Tanzania, and Sierra Leone. Zoe has also worked in operations, grant management, and monitoring and evaluation in Afghanistan and the Democratic Republic of Congo, and served in the Peace Corps as a small enterprise development volunteer in Senegal. She holds dual master's degrees in international affairs and journalism from Columbia University, and a bachelor's degree in foreign service from Georgetown University.

Victor Quiroz

Victor may not be an actual wizard, but he sure knows his way around an excel spreadsheet and datasets.

After completing a six-month internship with Whole Planet Foundation and graduating from St. Edward's University, Victor joined Whole Planet Foundation in September 2012.

Prior to working with the Foundation, he completed an internship in risk analysis and also gained experience writing grants for another local non-profit. Today, Victor supports Whole Planet Foundation's programs as our Data Analyst by collecting, sorting, and managing the data and information Whole Planet Foundation receives from its partners around the world.

Victor has also designed and implemented several tools that are designed to help the team manage our portfolio and visualize our data more effectively and efficiently.

Brian Doe

Brian was hired as the Africa Field Program Manager in 2010 to manage growing Whole Planet Foundation support in Africa, he is providing additional oversight to current microfinance partners and expanding WPF's work across the continent with new dynamic microfinance institutions.

Brian's first experience with Africa was building trade linkages in the private sector between businesses in West Africa and Illinois under a program funded by the Illinois state legislature in 1999, and he has been interested in finding better ways of linking the U.S. private and non-profit sectors with strong counterparts in Africa ever since.

He first travelled to the continent in 2000 as a Water and Sanitation volunteer with the Peace Corps in Mauritania (West Africa), and then moved his way into managing small grants and contracts to local partners for U.S. organizations working on the continent. To date, he has been fortunate to have worked closely with hundreds of different local NGOs and businesses in countries as diverse as the Congo, Sudan, Ethiopia, Kenya, Tunisia, and others.

Stephanie Manciagli

 Stephanie joined the team in 2019 as the Program Manager for Latin America & the Caribbean to support Whole Planet's implementing partners in carrying out their respective socially-focused microfinance programs.

While she was raised in Atlanta, Stephanie grew up in a multicultural household with each of her grandparents from a different country (United States, Jamaica, Italy and Canada). From Atlanta, Stephanie went on to get a B.A. in International Affairs at Florida State, spending 12 months of her studies in the Republic of Panama. After a term of service with AmeriCorps and working as a Program Coordinator for Points of Light, Stephanie returned to Panama as a graduate student through Tulane University, where she also worked as a Program Assistant at the United Nations Development Program. Following graduation, Stephanie moved to Paraguay and worked as Fundacion Paraguaya's Assistant Manager for the Poverty Stoplight. In this role, she coordinated the operations, programming and relationship-building for Poverty Stoplight's growing partnerships across 23 countries.

Having seen first-hand the impact that microlending has had (and having fallen in love with Latin America), Stephanie is inspired to be working out of Panama to support Whole Planet partners throughout the Caribbean, Central America and South America as they work hand in hand with entrepreneurs to build prosperity.

Joy Stoddard

Joy joined Whole Foods Market in 2000 and Whole Planet Foundation in 2006. In her role as the leader of Whole Planet Foundation's Development and Outreach Team, she develops strategic partnerships, connects people to our mission, and invites new advocates to join our cause.

Having traveled in 42 countries and 48 states, she is inspired to share the transformative power of microcredit and create prosperity. Joy has been awarded All*Star six times, Team Member of the Year and numerous leadership recognitions from Whole Foods Market. Previously, she coordinated training programs at the International Monetary Fund for six years. She has a B.A. from Washington and Lee University and speaks French and Spanish. Joy enjoys Austin with her husband Scott and teenager Roman.

Jason Martinez

Jason started his career at Whole Foods Market in 2013 and has been a huge advocate and supporter of Whole Planet Foundation since then. He travelled to Togo, West Africa as a Team Member Volunteer to see the Foundation's mission in action in 2016 and has shown up at nearly every single local event, always helpful, always keen to alleviate poverty for the world's poorest people. In 2017 he was inducted into the Whole Planet Foundation hall of fame inaugural class.

Jason is passionate about sports, playing soccer (first love), golf, tennis, volleyball and ping pong on a regular basis. He also loves to travel and has lived in Peru, South Korea, and the Czech Republic, while traveling to over 45 other countries. He's always excited to hear about your favorite places around the world or where you're headed next.

Genie Bolduc

Genie is the Global Educator for Whole Planet Foundation and the Whole Foods Market Team Member Volunteer Program Manager. Genie came to Whole Foods Market in Austin in 2002 and has held many positions at Whole Foods Market, from cashier to Store Trainer, to Associate Store Team Leader to Internal Programs Ambassador for Whole Planet Foundation in 2008.

In her current role she provides educational materials for Whole Planet Foundation and assists groups of Whole Foods Market Team Members in the opportunity to travel to places where Whole Foods Market sources products and Whole Planet Foundation funds microlending programs, to immerse themselves in global communities, becoming ambassadors for Whole Planet Foundation.

Through the program, Whole Foods Market Team Members broaden their horizons, participate in community service projects and learn about the transformative power of microcredit firsthand. Sharing the mission of Whole Planet Foundation with Whole Foods Market Team Members and helping to raise awareness and funds for poverty alleviation, is a dream job for her.

Sandy Mariscal

Sandy (left) is the Marketing and Outreach Program Manager for Whole Planet Foundation. She is responsible for the ongoing support and development of our Supplier Partnerships and general support of WPF programs.

A graduate of Santa Clara University, she holds a Bachelors in Sociology with a special emphasis in Business and Human Services and a Minor in Ethnic Studies. Prior to joining Whole Foods Market in 2008, Sandy worked as the Project Manager for Youth, Communities, and Social Justice Project at SCU and SFU. Native to the San Francisco Bay Area, she was fortunate to spend all her childhood summers in rural Corongoros, Mexico and is fluent in Spanish. Sandy has 19 years of retail grocery experience, 7 of which she worked as Marketing and Community Outreach Team Leader in Whole Foods Market's Norcal Region at Flagship Stevens Creek, Los Gatos, and Pioneer Palo Alto. In 2010, she pursued her passion for Whole Planet Foundation's mission and traveled as a Team Member volunteer to Arequipa, Peru. There she observed firsthand the extraordinary power of microcredit in action through microcredit lender Pro Mujer, helped build water cisterns for the community, and volunteered at the local school.

Over the years, she has helped support microloan fundraising through marketing activities like the Hustle for Whole Planet Run, community and team member presentations, and in-store events. Sandy is thrilled to be pursuing her passion for partnerships, cultural diversity, and Whole Planet Foundation in her current role to help alleviate poverty around the world in a sustainable way that empowers recipients, celebrates cultural differences, and respects different ways of life.

Jessica Villanueva

Jessica grew up in border city Juarez, Mexico. It was not until college that she moved to Austin, Texas to pursue a career in accounting. She has a Bachelors of Business Administration from Texas State University. Her goal was to find a niche in accounting for nonprofit and work for a company that mirrored her core values.

Jessica first joined Whole Foods Market Global Support as an Associate Accountant for the General Ledger Team, where she provided some accounting support to Whole Planet Foundation. She transitioned to the Whole Planet Foundation Team in early 2015 as the Administrator of Business & Finance and is now the Finance Coordinator for the foundation.

Like almost every Austinite, Jessica enjoys jogging around Town Lake with her dog, trying every food truck on her way, live music and festivals. She also enjoys playing, watching and having discussions about soccer.

Co-Editors and Contributors:

Olivia Hayden

Olivia is the co-editor of this book and has been on the Whole Planet Foundation team for almost five years. She designs and updates our website, manages our social media, email marketing, graphic design, and lends her creative eye toward many of the foundation's initiatives. She also brings Whole Planet Foundation's mission to life with videos from her visits to microfinance partners, both in the United States and abroad.

In 2006, Olivia joined Whole Foods Market and was part of the first Whole Planet Foundation Prosperity Campaign in stores, asking customers to donate to the mission at the registers. She was inspired by the stories of women starting businesses around the globe and set her sights on working toward purpose-driven and creative work. Almost 15 years later, she is proud to support the foundation's work as a Team Member.

Olivia graduated Summa Cum Laude with a BA in Communication Studies from Loyola Marymount University in Los Angeles, where she minored in Fine Arts. She is driven to bring new ideas to life through artistic pursuits. In her free time, she paints, crochets, refinishes antique furniture, dances at honky tonks, and enjoys the great outdoors in Austin, Texas.

Philip Sansone

Philip is the co-editor of this book and the founding President and Executive Director of Whole Planet Foundation, overseeing operations, programmatic direction and financial management. Philip brings over 50 years of expertise and experience to the mission and operations of the Foundation. His diverse and far ranging background focuses on three distinct arenas in international development: entrepreneurship, subsistence agricultural cooperatives and microfinance in developing countries.

As an entrepreneur in Austin, Texas, Philip founded Book People – one of the largest independent bookstores in the country. Philip was also the director of Multimedia, a business unit of Whole Foods Market's Wholepeople.com and importer of indigenous arts and crafts from the developing world. In the international development arena, Philip managed community development projects in Latin America for the Peace Corps and USAID and in Afghanistan for a non-governmental organization.

In the 1970s as a subsistence agricultural cooperative specialist, Philip worked for seven years with small subsistence farmers in Latin America and more recently in Afghanistan to encourage farmers to choose alternatives to the opium poppy cultivation. He was a Peace Corps Volunteer in Honduras where he worked with the Misquito Indians for almost three years on the Patuca River in La Mosquitia, and in Paraguay for four years helping to start agricultural cooperatives.

Part I:

FINANCIAL INCLUSION

Chapter 1

Access to Finance in Senegal
By Brian Doe

Noel (far right in the photo above) borrows about $800 to stock her market stand in Senegal's central Kaolack Market. Her current loan is her sixth with the microfinance institution (MFI) CAURIE, in Senegal.

When asked where she had gotten her stock, (you can see her shelves are packed with items for sale) she picked up some fabric and recounted how she had gone by local bus from Senegal, across West Africa and on to Cameroon and Chad to buy the fabric in bulk. She traveled for days each way to amass inventory that would diversify her stall's stock of goods.

Digging deeper into her inventory as her story piqued my interest, I learned she had buckets of incenses from Saudi Arabia (which she bought during her recent Muslim Hajj (pilgrimage) and piles of high-quality fabric and clothing from Mali, Burkina Faso and Togo. Noel said she had also once been to China to buy beauty and body products to then resell in this market stall in Kaolack.

Adding up the cost of travel, shipping, and logistics it would take to run this kind of business and estimating the value of her inventory, I realized that the cash flow going through this small market stall was likely in the thousands of dollars.

Yet Noel is financing the growth of her business from a microfinance institution like CAURIE which has an average loan size available for local entrepreneurs of just $200. CAURIE is stretched to offer any business loans greater than $1000. Additionally, CAURIE needs all loans to be repaid within six months.

Why is Noel borrowing from CAURIE when she has enough collateral to certainly back a much larger loan from a larger formal bank?

When asked why she wasn't borrowing from a bank, Noel said she had gone through the requirements once to take a loan from a formal bank through a special business loan fund specifically for small and medium enterprises. However, the bank was so unprepared to work with small-scale businesses that it actually required 200 Kaolack women to apply together for a single bank business loan. The group ended up with a loan among them of about $58,000, of which for Noel received business capital of just $500. To make it worse, she said the loan was more expensive than CAURIE and was certainly more difficult to apply for.

A MICROCREDIT GROUP MEETING OF CAURIE IN SENEGAL

CAURIE is a Senegalese NGO offering start-up capital to rural women micro-entrepreneurs but is now finding itself as one of the few financial service resources for the region's rural business sector and for very small-scale businesses. Unfortunately, CAURIE is only rarely offered the quantities of loan capital necessary to serve more than the most basic rural business clients with very small amounts of business capital.

This is a lesson on how detached the mainstream financial services sector remains from the population in this community (and many others- and in many other countries besides Senegal): A woman running a high value and sophisticated commerce business has borrowed and repaid business loans successfully 5 times but still cannot access sufficient business finance to grow apart from the loans of a grassroots village banking program like CAURIE.

Chapter 2

Adding Value in Sri Lanka: Berendina's Enterprise Development Services (EDS)

By Claire Kelly

Providing access to credit is the fundamental service of all of Whole Planet Foundation's microfinance partners. But what is the best way to support borrowers as they use their loan capital to start or grow a small business? This is actually a very difficult question.

Client trainings can augment the investment that clients can make in their business, but they cost money to implement. To cover the costs of client trainings, a microfinance institution (MFI) may need to raise interest rates or add fees. And perhaps there are some clients who would prefer to pay a cheaper price for the loan rather than pay for trainings that may or may not be applicable to their business needs. In addition to increased costs, clients may end up forced to waste their valuable time in a training that somebody else has decided is valuable.

WPF's microfinance partner in Sri Lanka, Berendina (BMI), addresses this challenge with a market-driven training program called Enterprise Development Services (EDS). According to BMI's annual report, "The objective of the EDS service is to ensure the long-term sustainability and growth of the borrowers' business ventures by developing a wide variety of their skills, which primarily include their technical skills, business management skills and financial literacy."

Clients choose which trainings they would like to attend, and then pay for their desired training sessions. Berendina staff therefore has to respond to client demand for high quality support on topics the clients feel can develop their businesses.

Berendina has developed 3 types of client support Enterprise Development Services:

Type A EDS
This includes technical training (e.g.: sewing, food processing & preservation), agriculture training (e.g.: poultry management, composting) and financial literacy. These trainings focus mostly on teaching or developing

skills that clients can use as income-generating activities. At the loan disbursement, borrowers are issued coupons valued from 1200-2500 LKR (about $8-16USD), depending on the size of the loan. The total value of the coupons is repaid over the course of the loan along with the principal and interest payments for the loan.

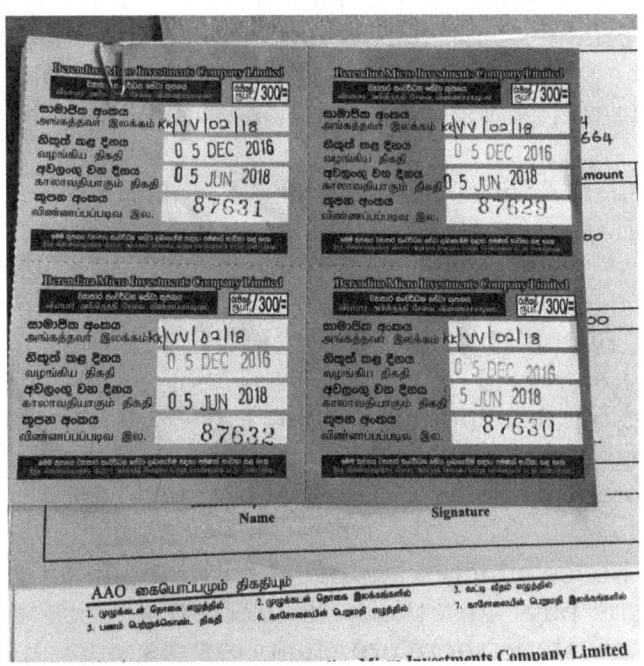

AN EXAMPLE OF THE COUPONS BMIC CLIENTS RECEIVE AT LOAN DISBURSEMENT

The borrower can redeem the coupons for participation in various trainings, depending on her preferences. For example, the clients in the photo below each paid 4 coupons (1200 LKR, which is about $8) to participate in a sewing training. The cost covered 2 full days of instruction from a local specialist (resource person), materials for the course, and meals each day. If the borrower doesn't wish to participate in any training during the loan cycle, she can cash in the coupons at face value at the end of the cycle towards the repayment of the last installment.

Each Berendina branch has one EDS officer who is in charge of running the program. The EDS officer gets feedback from the clients about what trainings they are interested in and s/he uses this information to register qualified resource people into the pool of Berendina instructors. Then the EDS officer works with the microfinance officers to promote the upcoming courses and organize the event. EDS is especially popular in the WPF-supported Kaliwanchikudy branch, thanks in large part to the dedicated staff there. At this point, Berendina has made a gross profit from the direct services and the entire program is 80% self-sufficient.

COUPONS CAN BE REDEEMED FOR TYPE A TECHNICAL TRAININGS (SEWING)

Type B EDS (Business Support)

Clients can also receive individualized assistance from their Berendina Enterprise Development Officer. Typical business support services include helping a client to register her business, helping a client to sign up for livestock insurance or giving business advice on advertising. While the technical trainings require coupons, the Type B and Type C EDS services are offered free of charge as a benefit to Berendina members.

RANJINI MEETS WITH OTHER CLIENTS WHO ARE ALL INVOLVED IN PALMERA WEAVING AS PART OF TYPE C EDS (MARKET LINKAGES)

Type C EDS (Special Income Generating Projects)

Berendina members who participate in the same type of enterprise also come together periodically as part of Type C EDS. While the members in the photo below belong to different cluster groups for their borrowing, they all weave natural baskets from Palmera leaves. This group can have more business opportunities when united together. For example, they can organize to buy raw materials in bulk, market their products, design and share new models (such as woven flowerpots) and link up with other support services.

Berendina has also organized events like craft fairs to showcase artisan products of different types, including the Palmera products. While some clients weave baskets as a main livelihood activity, most weave Palmera products as a side project. For example, Ranjini (pictured in orange below) does tailoring for her main income generating activity. (She is in her first loan cycle with BMIC, borrowing 30,000 LKR, approximately $200.) However, she also produces about 3 or 4 baskets on the side for some extra income every week. According to Ranjini, it is the training provided by Berendina's EDS program that really makes the loan capital useful.

Access to loan capital alone is only one way to help micro-entrepreneurs build a business that will provide income for themselves and their family. They also need access to other tools like savings accounts, insurance, technical assistance and training. Berendina's EDS methodology is an excellent example of an innovative model providing support in a sustainable *and* client-centric way.

Chapter 3

Broadening Financial Inclusion Borders in Bangladesh: Spotlight on Whole Planet's Bold, New Partnerships

By Claire Kelly

According to Women's World Banking, "Women in Bangladesh have the highest-ever rates of literacy and employment, and the country's economy is growing. Financial inclusion now stands at more than 50 percent, nearly doubling in the past few years. But the financial inclusion gender gap is growing rapidly too, with fewer than half of women accessing or using formal financial services."

This is a surprising trend from the country widely considered to be the birthplace of microfinance. While the sector is characterized by many nationally scaled financing programs, many have not innovated product offerings in response to clients, especially women clients' needs. While the Women's World Banking article highlights opportunities for further behavioral research to answer these questions, WPF can spotlight two new Bangladesh partnerships, started in 2016, which provide adapted products and services for women and likewise stretch the borders of traditional microfinance.

BRAC's Ultra-Poor Graduation Programme

The first is BRAC's Ultra-Poor Graduation (UPG) programme (previously known as Targeting the Ultra Poor (TUP) Programme. While WPF's microfinance partners typically use various targeting methods to identify low-income people to join their program, a microloan is not suitable for somebody who is very poor, or "ultra-poor." A microloan needs to be invested in an income-generating project so that the borrower can generate profit and be able to pay back the loan and interest. However, an ultra-poor individual has immediate needs for basics such as food and shelter that would likely divert microloan funds from business investment to personal needs. Also, the ultra-poor individual may lack self-confidence about their repayment capacity.

UPG is a comprehensive, time-bound, integrated and sequenced set of interventions that includes a) a high value asset package or capital of grant and/or interest free loan, b) enterprise development training, c)hands-on coaching, d) matched savings, e) healthcare services and f) community mobilization support that aims to enable ultra-poor households to achieve key milestones towards sustainable livelihoods and socioeconomic resilience, and progress along a pathway out of extreme poverty.

SUJATA IS A MICROCREDIT CLIENT OF BRAC IN BANGLADESH

WPF has supported four such graduation-from-poverty projects, as of March 2019, in our global portfolio. With BRAC-UPG, WPF funds were dedicated towards the grant component of the business asset for these participants. At BRAC-UPG three types of assets (livestock, agriculture and non-farm enterprise) are provided to the participants. These typically have a purchase price of 20,000 Taka ($237 USD) maximum. For example, the most popular asset is a dairy cow, and for the most vulnerable participants, half of these funds are provided as a grant while the others are given them as an interest-free loan to be repaid by the participant. Less vulnerable participants receive smaller grant amounts and repay a larger portion; different enterprise selections also have different loan/grant breakdowns.

At BRAC-UPG, participants must complete a minimum of five mandatory criteria and get at least 7 out of the 10 points for other criteria to graduate. 95% of the participants graduate from the program within the two-year period. Participants are also better linked with financial services. All participants open a savings account and practice regular savings with a local group called a Village Organization (VO). Furthermore, many participants take a microfinance loan after the two-year UPG intervention.

"Credit-Plus" Lending with "SUPPORT"

While UPG brings those below the microfinance entry point into the financial inclusion ladder, WPF's other partner in Bangladesh, SUPPORT, has an innovation for businesses that have successfully grown from the microenterprise stage to the small enterprise stage. WPF works with microfinance partner SUPPORT to finance their loan portfolio in two branches in the northern regions' Char areas.

SUPPORT has partnered with Oxfam to offer financing to women who have participated in their dairy enterprise training and market linkage program. The microloan is used to finance a high yield milch cow, which will produce more milk; when linked with the forward market systems such as chilling centers and processing plants, the borrowers get access to formal buyers as well. SUPPORT will finance these women-led dairy enterprises up to 50,000 Taka (≈$590), which goes towards the purchase of a crossbreed (higher quality) cow. The borrowers we visited already had 1 or 2 local-breed cows, but with the training and increased market linkage options provided together with the financing from SUPPORT, the clients invested in the higher quality crossbreed cows. These crossbreed cows produce milk up to four times what a local breed produces, so there are many opportunities to substantially grow their businesses. Once a client has four cows, she can consider a different loan product to install a bio-digester for a more environmentally friendly, healthier cooking and energy option.

WHOLE PLANET FOUNDATION VISITS A MEETING OF SUPPORT STAFF AND CLIENTS

While the dairy value chain partnership leverages several market actors to bring up the level of these microfinance borrowers, SUPPORT has another innovation. They are

40

a member of a larger umbrella organization called STEPs. SUPPORT MFI builds their branches together with other STEPs members, in moving from a microcredit branch to a Financial Inclusion Center (FIC). SUPPORT MFI clients come to the FICs for a host of services like loan disbursements, bank accounts, technical assistance, financial literacy trainings, and more.

SUPPORT registers borrowers on the i-SME platform of STEPs partner organization, Bangladesh SME Corporation Limited (BSCL). The i-SME platform prompts Field Officers to ask customers detailed questions about their overall business activities, revenues, assets, inventory, profit margins etc. in an informal way. Staff use the i-SME tool to input client information, which then builds a financial profile of the enterprise along with a credit score. Time-series data is subsequently captured over the tenor of the loan as the business and repayment history is built and recorded. The borrower is then able to leverage this credit history in the future to qualify for a bank loan application through an Agent Bank (also located within the FICs).

This is a significant step towards longer-term sustainability, because bank loans are less expensive than microfinance loans. However, often clients with higher capacity and capital needs stay within the microfinance sector because typical banks lack the outreach infrastructure for a credit assessment. The innovative i-SME platform extends financial inclusion by helping the under-served micro-borrowers to graduate from microfinance and access larger capital at cheaper rates.

In addition to leveraging Oxfam's dairy value chain capacity building and BSCL's investor-investee matchmaking platform (the i-SME), SUPPORT has another client-centric feature. Financial Inclusion Centers provide "tele-medicine" services to the beneficiaries, which is an opportunity for clients (especially women) to connect via a video portal with a qualified female doctor based in the capital city of Dhaka. The patients are able to access high quality medical advice without travel time and expense. A personalized prescription is automatically printed out at the end of the session to purchase any required medicines from a pharmacy.

Layering financial services with livelihood assistance and community-building services such as healthcare and business counseling are innovative approaches by both BRAC UPG and SUPPORT. Often referred to as credit-plus microfinance, this approach is a typical characteristic across Whole Planet Foundation's global portfolio.

Chapter 4

Financial Diaries: Lessons from Small Enterprise Foundation in South Africa

By Zoe So

WHOLE PLANET FOUNDATION VISITS A MEETING OF SMALL ENTERPRISE
FOUNDATION IN SOUTH AFRICA

One of the core assumptions of microfinance is that the ability to reach a large number of borrowers helps bring efficiencies, sustainability, and impact. Many microfinance organizations often talk about their success in terms of scale and big picture numbers: how many borrowers do they reach? How big has their loan portfolio grown?

But MFIs need to answer a different set of questions to develop a more granular understanding of their impact on a household level: What do their clients' lives look like? What are their various sources of income? What do they spend money on, and how do they make those decisions? How do they handle paying for emergencies? What strategies do they use to manage their finances and to save?

A fuller picture of a family's financial circumstances can help MFIs improve the design and delivery of their financial services.

How Financial Diaries Can Help

MFIs are increasingly using detailed case studies to get at such questions by applying a research methodology called financial diaries. Researchers visit the same families regularly over a period of time to collect detailed information about each household's financial activities, coupled with questions about financial behavior. Financial diaries were pioneered and popularized by the book Portfolios of the Poor (required reading for all WPF staff!). Since then this approach has gained traction as a tool to better understand financial insecurity and decision-making in households throughout the world, including in the US.

"The Financial Diaries: How American Families Cope in a World of Uncertainty," reveals findings from an in-depth study tracking one year of financial transactions of 235 low- to moderate-income families, from four different communities in the U.S. The researchers found that many families faced income volatility throughout the year, making financial planning difficult and creating situations where families sometimes had to borrow money at an expensive rate, potentially leading to indebtedness.

Small Enterprise Foundation (SEF), our partner in South Africa, recently completed their own financial diaries study which looked at how 41 clients used their micro-loans by tracking their financial income and expenditures. SEF, whose clients are all low-income women, states that the goal of this study was to "shed light on the positive aspects of client impact as well as guide us on how to better improve ways to achieve our social mission."

From June 2015 to December 2015, SEF researchers visited the selected households once every two weeks. The key findings from their study are:

- Business income universally added to household income
- However, clients had varying ability to use a loan from SEF to support income-generating activities
- Clients who already had an established business before taking the loan tended to be more successful than those who did not.
- For the loan takers who were less successful in converting a loan to an income generating business, some of the challenges included:
  - Difficulty generating business ideas
  - Challenge with local market cash flows (for example, selling on credit was followed by clients' inability to recuperate owed payments.)

Financial diaries yield rich household-level information; yet there are some caveats to the approach. For example, the sample size is generally small, and the households selected may not be representative of the wider population. The repeated visits can come with a high demand on the time of participating households, and participants may drop out. The goal of this approach is to apply rigorous analysis to uncover deep, rather than broad, insights.

For Small Enterprise Foundation, the financial diaries may help inform several initiatives under development. As of June 2018, they were updating and refining a questionnaire, administered at each loan, to better understand the level of poverty of client relative to the local context. They're also looking at improving ways to deliver business skills training to clients.

Chapter 5

Financial Inclusion for What?
Celebrating Financial Inclusion
Week with a Profile of CASHPOR

By Claire Kelly

During 2019's *Financial Inclusion Week*, Accion's Center for Financial Inclusion asked, *"Financial Inclusion for What?"* In other words: what are the main goals that financial inclusion is striving to achieve?

Whole Planet Foundation has been a unique capital provider in the financial inclusion space for more than 15 years. The foundation provides free capital to many organizations that are operating sustainably. Therefore, WPF selects partners with a strong social focus in terms of the implementation of financial services and other services that can be delivered to clients by leveraging their field-based microcredit programs. WPF evaluates partners on their ability to provide accessible, transparent, affordable and supportive services to their clients.

Within Accion's framework – this would translate to:

1. Financial inclusion for financial health
2. Financial inclusion for equity
3. Financial inclusion for sustainable development.

CASHPOR: A Case Study

During a 2019 monitoring and evaluation trip, I visited one of WPF's microfinance partners in India, CASHPOR. They are an excellent model for the types of microfinance institutions (MFIs) that can leverage WPF capital in an extremely effective way towards these three targets.

Financial Inclusion for Financial Health

"Fundamentally, financial tools exist to help people manage mismatches between their income and expenses over time and space and build lump sums of cash. The ability to do those things can be thought of as financial health." -From Accion's Center for Financial Inclusion

In the Indian context, there is no shortage of credit providers who are willing to offer loans. CASHPOR has taken the approach under their New Growth Strategy to finance the full, legitimate capital needs of their borrowers. In return, the borrowers are asked to borrow exclusively from CASHPOR. This strategy recognizes that clients have both business credit needs as well as family credit needs (like school fees, marriages or illnesses) that require access to lump sums. CASHPOR's flexibility in amount and purpose of their microloans allows borrowers to manage their cash flows, take advantage of business opportunities and respond to emergencies. CASHPOR gives the loans with full context of the entire family's repayment capacity and by working exclusively with CASHPOR, the risk of over-indebtedness, which is associated with multiple loans, can be decreased.

Financial Inclusion for Equity

Accion asserts microfinance institutions *"should be striving for equity – fair access, fair use and fair treatment for customers – but where do we focus our efforts?"*

CASHPOR CLIENT, INDRAWATI, AND HER TWO DAUGHTERS

These first two ideas of financial health and financial equity are very closely linked for an organization like CASHPOR. It is impossible even to describe CASHPOR's provision of financial services to smooth capital needs without discussing how they are providing capital in a responsible way. These two goals are fundamentally linked.

In terms of fair access, it is significant to look at CASHPOR's target population. The organization works in 5 of the poorest states in India. Within these states, they focus on rural areas and use tools such as the CASHPOR Housing Index to specifically prioritize Below Poverty Line (BPL) households. According to CASHPOR's stats almost 90% of members are from "scheduled castes, scheduled tribes or other backward classes."

In terms of usage, CASHPOR strives to offer the lowest interest rates in the areas which they serve. Fair treatment of customers is taken especially seriously by the CASHPOR staff.

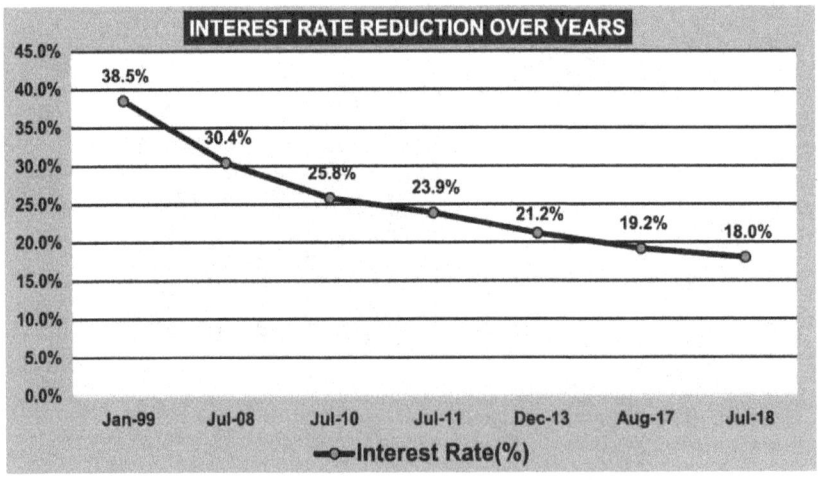

CASHPOR STRIVES TO OFFER THE LOWEST INTEREST RATES IN THE AREAS WHICH THEY SERVE

While most WPF partners make a point to print branch and regional staff phone contacts on passbooks or even have a head office hotline where complaints can be filed,

CASHPOR goes even further to have a "Client Satisfaction Day." On the 15th of every month, clients are encouraged to visit the branch office and discuss any concerns or feedback they have.

Financial Inclusion for Sustainable Development

"Financial inclusion, financial services, and microfinance are explicitly mentioned in the targets of seven of the 17 Sustainable Development Goals. Their presence implies that financial services are a means to improve quality of life and suggests that creating financial stability should not be the only goal of financial inclusion." - Accion's Center for Financial Inclusion

Indeed, CASHPOR's vision and mission go beyond providing financial services but also to deliver health and education services as approaches to break the intergenerational poverty cycle of the clients they serve. CASHPOR leverages its rural network to provide access to these services. One key to CASHPOR's health and education initiatives is a team of more than 3,000 Community Health Facilitators which cover about 95% of CASHPOR's centers! These are CASHPOR clients who have gone through intensive training and internship in partnership with Healing Fields Foundation and now deliver health modules to their fellow clients. CHFs also take on additional roles in the organization, like promoting health-related loans and monitoring educational activities that keep these programs scaled across the large organization.

A health catastrophe can be a big setback to a low-income client. CHFs maximize the time that clients come together on a weekly basis for their credit and saving activities to deliver preventative trainings. CHFs also sell health-related items like insect repellent and sanitary napkins. And they promote products such as the sanitation loan, in which CASHPOR will provide financing for the construction of a toilet at the client's home. CASHPOR also leverages its rural branches to deliver Mini Health Clinics where doctors visit twice a month to provide consultations and medicine. As of March 2019, 177 CASHPOR branches held mini-health clinics, serving almost 134,000 clients.

While a health catastrophe can send a rising client back into poverty, educational opportunities are a strong way to propel a family forward. CASHPOR's specific goal is that every family should have at least one child pass the grade 10 exams, which unlocks the possibility for government jobs. To this end, CASHPOR has partnered with an NGO named PRATHAM to develop Education Centers where students can get tutoring before or after regular school hours. CASHPOR has established 1,092 .CASHPOR Educational Centers which serve over 33,000 students. As of most recently available info, 93% of the CEC students who sat for the class 10 exam in Bihar and Uttar Pradesh have passed. Clients pay a small amount for participation in the education centers and/or health clinics in order to recoup some of the costs and continue to scale the programs. The CHFs earn stipends from CASHPOR for their work.

Historically, subordinated debt and grant capital from donors like WPF reinforce CASHPOR's capital which, in turn, unlocks their ability to take on further borrowing. As CASHPOR has become more sophisticated, they can expand their program directly by employing funds from their banking correspondent partners to entire branches. However, fresh funds from WPF can be leveraged for the riskier expansion areas where CASHPOR has traditionally used their own funds to grow. Because of the non-profit structure, income earned from interest is all reinvested back into the organization – helping CASHPOR to continue to expand their financial and non-financial services. Operational efficiencies are then shared back with clients through reducing interest rates over time. (And in 2018 – an interest refund to veteran clients!)

Whether large or small, WPF seeks out partners with responsible finance practices and the ability to use WPF funds in an impactful way. In addition to supporting traditional socially focused MFI's like CASHPOR, WPF's mandate also incorporates other innovative approaches such as the Ultra Poor graduation framework and social enterprises providing clean energy and health products on credit.

Chapter 6

Productive Assets Spell Success for Entrepreneurs in Africa

By Brian Doe

BRAC UGANDA CLIENT LOY WITH HER PRODUCTIVE ASSETS: CALVES

Many of the borrowers we support in Africa use their business loan capital to buy something in bulk and resell it at a mark-up that repays the loan and leaves some profit with the entrepreneur.

This is a low-risk business strategy that returns the loan capital fairly easily and quickly, allowing the entrepreneur to repay her loan in time. However, the profit comes in very small margins.

Whole Planet Foundation's Programs team has analyzed the importance of productive assets to microcredit client businesses in Africa. 'Productive assets' are things that help create income for a business owner without needing to sell the asset itself. If an entrepreneur invests in a larger asset like a vehicle, plow, sewing machine, refrigerator or other equipment, the possibility for higher profit can be transformative over time.

We have several partners in Zambia, Madagascar and East Africa focusing more exclusively on the procurement and sale, on affordable terms, of these productive assets to entrepreneurs in rural areas.

Loy's Story

Take Loy, a client who I met in Uganda who is pictured at the top of this chapter. She took out a business loan of about $175 with our microfinance partner BRAC Uganda's youth loan program and used it to buy calves. She resells the cows when they are grown and has been repeating this process over and over for the past three years.

After we went inside Loy's house, she showed me a recent new addition to the business, thanks to a program launched by BRAC Uganda. The program allows youth participants to boost income through access to various productive assets combined with training.

In Loy's case, she received a sewing machine and sewing training. This has allowed her to make steadier and larger profits from her work repairing and tailoring clothes. Self-employment for rural youth is an area of enormous need in a country like Uganda, with 78 percent of the population under 30 and youth making up 64 percent of the unemployed workforce.

Loy was qualified to receive a subsidized sewing machine through BRAC Uganda's program, in which select participants obtain assets for free or at reduced costs. However, for most businesswomen it would be very hard to buy a sewing machine with a loan term of 6-12 months and actually earn enough from the machine to pay for the loan. Even if a client could repay the loan, it would be difficult to make enough additional profit to support her other expenses before the loan came fully due.

This is one of many reasons it can often be very hard for clients to invest in productive assets, but think of the opportunities that entrepreneurs are missing out on:

- A farmer growing maize could earn more with a mill to grind it into flour.
- A woman selling clothes could earn more if she could build a shop in the central market area.
- A person selling vegetables could sell twice as much if she could buy a truck or cart to transport the stock to and from her rural markets.

Productive Assets Spell Success

Whole Planet Foundation's team in Africa has been very focused on testing ways our partners (or possibly complementary partnerships with other social ventures) can help meet business owners' needs for productive assets.

In Zambia, the Whole Planet Foundation supports a social business called Rent to Own, which offers larger assets on a repayment plan. Rent to Own also includes the procurement, delivery and set-up of assets like this solar pump pictured below, purchased by one client who can now support year-round vegetable gardening in addition to a seasonal maize crop.

A CLIENT OF RENT TO OWN ZAMBIA WITH HIS SOLAR PUMP

Our partners in East Africa are also looking into offering similar access to productive assets, though still at a much smaller and more basic level for now. There is still a lot of work to do in getting significant assets like these into the hands of poor business owners. Most asset and equipment purchasing programs remain accessible only to larger businesses.

In the meantime, Whole Planet Foundation has continued to support institutions that also offer their clients the ability to save money in addition to providing small business loans. Maintaining savings can be the best way for business owners earning small profits to keep some funds aside to eventually invest in productive assets like buildings and equipment.

Whole Planet Foundation's team in Africa works with microfinance partners to ensure microentrepreneurs have the option to receive beneficial loan products and productive assets. We have seen the impact that access to large productive assets can have on client businesses first-hand and look forward to working with our partners to find solutions that will increase access for generations to come.

Chapter 7

Credit-Plus Spotlight: Savings

How Whole Planet's MFI Partners Provide Access and Support for Client Savings

By Claire Kelly

MICROCREDIT CLIENTS OF CASHPOR IN INDIA

WPF funds are provided to our partner microfinance institutions (MFIs) to be distributed to borrowers as microloans or in-kind productive assets (like cows, sewing machines, or solar lamps).   For most of our partners, the loan is given in a "credit-plus" context. This means that the MFI would provide supportive financial and/or nonfinancial products as well as credit.

Types of supportive financial products that various partners offer are savings, financial literacy, insurance, business development, agriculture market linkages and links to bank accounts and loans at more formal institutions. Nonfinancial services can range from health/life-skills trainings, access to clean energy products, health clinics, scholarships and tutoring for clients' children and vocational skills training. None of our partners provide all of these services, but each partner provides the wrap-around support that they can, given: the regulations in the country, the partner's expertise, access to funds and their balance of the costs clients pay and their expectations of high quality service.

In this cross-regional blog, we're taking a deep dive into savings and what this looks like across various partners in the WPF MFI network. Our microfinance partners typically promote savings in one of four ways:
- Promoting savings within the graduation program
- Strengthening Savings and Loan Groups (SLG's) where clients save informally within their community
- Linking clients to bank accounts at formal institutions
- Directly providing savings services to clients

Building the Savings Habit as Part of the Graduation Program

WPF has recently extended our support from MFIs to also include the Graduation methodology, a comprehensive, targeted and time-bound approach to reach households who are too poor to invest loan capital in a business. Forming clients into Savings and Loan Groups (SLGs) is typically a key step (among many) in this methodology.

Fonkoze in Haiti

For example, WPF supports Fonkoze Foundation's Chemen Lavi Miyò (CLM), or "Pathway to a Better Life" program. Regarding the savings component of CLM, Fonkoze Foundation received training in the SLG methodology from CARE International. In Haiti, these (SLG) associations consist of 20-30 neighbors who meet weekly for a year.

At each meeting, members buy from one to five shares at a price that the group itself sets at its first meeting. The money from share purchases then becomes a loan fund. Members can borrow up to three times their savings, repaying the loans with interest over three or five months. At the end of the year, each member receives her savings along with the profit the SLG has earned by making loans. All CLM members are organized into SLGs during the early months of the 18-month CLM graduation program. The associations are popular among CLM members, their case managers, and other members of the community who participate.

Leveraging Client Savings through SLGs

In Bangladesh, BRAC's Ultra Poor Graduation (UPG) also utilize SLG type groups called Village Organizations, (VO's). While BRAC used to provide stipends to the UPG participants as one component of the graduation package, they shifted towards the current iteration of matching client savings to link these vulnerable households' need for consumption support while promoting savings.

BRAC ULTRA-POOR GRADUATION PROGRAMME PARTICIPANTS' MEETING IN
BANGLADESH

One of the defining features of SLGs is that once properly formed and trained, they can operate independently of NGOs and MFIs. Many of WPF's partners leverage SLGs as part of their own group-based lending methodology. The linkage is not necessary for the SLG to function, but it can provide enhanced services. Just as a linkage between a SLG and MFI can provide access to a greater choice of loan products (such as larger capital amounts with longer repayment periods), the MFI can also support the savings activities of the SLG. And according to research published recently by the SEEP Network, combining savings groups with other economic development activity creates a greater likelihood of various empowerment outcomes for women compared to stand alone savings groups.

For example, WPF's partner Small Enterprise Development (SED) in Thailand was founded by Catholic Relief Services and therefore all their loan groups operate under a SLG model. SED provides ongoing technical assistance to the SLG's management committee to encourage proper fund management. SED also leverages their software system to calculate the distribution of SLG profits based on the amount each member has contributed as savings during the year. Lastly SED encourages the SLG to allocate a part of their annual savings dividend into initiatives such as compensation for the group management committee, buying productive

A CAJA RURAL IN HONDURAS

assets for the SLG, establishing group funds for loan default and group welfare.

In Latin America, WPF's MFI partner FUNDER works closely with the "Cajas Rurales" (type of SLG in Honduras). One of the technical components that FUNDER covers is calculating a sustainable and viable interest rate for the SLG. When MFIs strengthen the methodologies and capacity of the SLGs, it keeps the groups running smoothly and ensures that clients can continue to grow their savings with this approach.

MFIs Linking Clients to Traditional Banks

While some partners leverage informal SLGs as a way for clients to save, other WPF partners link clients to traditional banks to access savings services. The availability of traditional banks willing to partner with MFIs depends on the country and regional context.

However, in India for example, there is a big push from the government for banks to do "priority sector lending." One way for banks to meet these targets is to provide funds to MFIs who then manage these additional funds like their normal group lending.

As part of this partnership, our MFI partner CASHPOR and their banking correspondent (BC) partners also established a way for these clients to easily save with the BC banks as well. This is a value-added service for the CASHPOR clients because with the status of an NGO, CASHPOR is not permitted to collect savings directly.

MFIs Directly Providing Savings Services

Offering savings services directly usually requires a sophisticated organization who has received a deposit-taking license from the appropriate regulator. The requirements for this type of status vary tremendously from country to country, but usually the MFI would have to prove the strength of their own financial institution before the government agrees that the MFI should be trusted with a client's hard-earned savings.

As our network of MFIs typically run on very tight margins, trying to provide quality loan services at the lowest prices, it can take years to build up the capital requirements that are often necessary to become a regulated deposit-taking institution.

For example, WPF partnered with BRAC Uganda starting in 2010 and they have just recently transformed into a fully deposit-taking institution as of this post's writing in 2019.

When permitted to do so, some MFI partners have integrated savings directly into their methodology. For example, WPF's partner in Bhutan, RENEW Microfinance, was founded in collaboration with the German Savings Banks Foundation for International Cooperation (SBFIC) and offers a savings-led approach to microfinance. In Bhutan, clients must first slowly save for up to three months before they can access a loan. During the savings period, clients participate in financial literacy sessions. The idea is for RENEW to promote savings and

RENEW'S NEW PASSBOOKS RECORD CLIENT SAVINGS AND LOANS. (THEY'RE MADE FROM TRADITIONAL BHUTANESE FABRIC WOVEN BY RENEW NGO MEMBERS.

financial literacy to very rural areas where people don't otherwise have easy access to a bank. And RENEW pays 5% on all client deposits. After establishing savings services, those clients who need additional business capital are eligible to borrow a loan. Currently, only about 20% of RENEW's members are active borrowers.

In West Africa, many of WPF's partners have a long history of offering direct savings services. Like RENEW, the Entrepreneurs du Monde network programs such as

Yikri in Burkina Faso and ID Ghana usually integrate small, incremental, mandatory savings as a component of their loan programs. Premiere Agence de Microfinance (PAMF) in Cote d'Ivoire and GHAPE in Cameroon heavily promote voluntary savings to their members.

THE ELEPHANT SAVINGS PASSBOOK HELPS MICROCREDIT CLIENTS OF WFDF IN LAOS SAVE TO EDUCATE THEIR CHILDREN

Voluntary savings can be further promoted with special purpose savings. Another SBFIC supported MFI, WFDF in Laos, promotes voluntary savings by offering special purpose accounts. The "Elephant Savings" product is a special account where WFDF clients can save for their children's education. WFDF issues special passbooks (with the elephant and rainbow on the cover) and they are very popular! KOMIDA in Indonesia offers a popular feast-day savings product, where clients receive a lower interest rate if they agree to lock-in savings in preparation for holiday expenditures.

Links to Savings Set up Clients for Success

MFI focus on savings can be a great building block for financial literacy and further credit-plus services. And when such a socially focused, deposit-taking MFI still has a shortfall of loan capital, WPF funds can help fill that gap. However, if the MFI is very successful at collecting deposits, then they don't necessarily need the loan capital that WPF provides. Therefore, many of our MFI partners access free capital from WPF exactly because they lack the sophistication of a deposit-taking institution.

Perhaps they do not have the authority to collect savings in their country, or the total savings collected from the populations they serve is much smaller than their clients' demand for loans, or in some cases the microfinance provider itself has formed from a massively grown SLG/cooperative structure and therefore profits are distributed back to clients annually rather than reinvested in the portfolio. In any of these cases, the socially focused MFIs can still provide savings services to customers by creative links with SLGs or banks.

Chapter 8

The Importance of Savings in Burkina Faso

By Brian Doe

Madeleine, pictured here, is the President of one of Yikri's microfinance groups in Burkina Faso. She has successfully taken business loans to support livestock rearing activities. However, when explaining the difference the Yikri program had made in her life, she first recounted not the impact of credit on her economic situation but the importance of the savings accounts Yikri provides.

Launched by the French network Entrepreneurs du Monde, Yikri is one of Whole Planet Foundation's microfinance partners, part of a network we work with all around the globe to fund microcredit to the world's poor. Although Whole Planet Foundation provides capital to finance microloans to entrepreneurs in poor communities around the world, we know credit is only one part of a complex financial support system that can improve the lives of poor households.

MADELINE RAISES PIGS WITH A MICROLOAN FROM YIKRI IN BURKINA FASO

Prior to joining her Yikri group, Madeleine participated in a traditional savings method within her village where savings are collected and kept by a member of the community. One day, she lost everything she had saved when that collector's house burned down. After that experience, she remembered trying to save her money with a local savings and credit company that ended up going out of business and ultimately paid out a fraction of the money she had saved at the institution over time. Despite how successful her enterprise was, she found herself back to zero economically because she couldn't reliably save for the future and build the funds she needed to cover larger investments in her business and household.

Research into the impact of the microfinance sector has shown that stand alone, 'one size fits all' microlending programs are not as effective as those that provide credit flexible to borrowers' needs. Flexible business loans layered with easily accessible savings services, training, and when possible, more advanced products like insurance and asset leasing have more potential for sustainable economic empowerment of the poor.

The Harvard Business Review wrote in 2016 to highlight this research: "Recent evidence suggests that relatively simple tweaks to microcredit products—including flexible repayment periods, grace periods, individual-liability contracts, or the use of technology—may change their impact on poverty and financial institutions' bottom line."

Having just returned from a visit to Burkina Faso to observe the operations of WPF's partner Entrepreneurs du Monde, no organization seems to have been so responsive to these recommendations. Entrepreneurs du Monde, through their 'Yikri' microfinance program, does provide microloans to thousands of micro-enterprises in Burkina Faso (and other countries), but every enterprise supported is assessed independently and the repayment period is set up in collaboration with the entrepreneur to be appropriate to the business activity. Loans can vary from 3 months to 12 months and there is a possibility for a grace period until the end of the loan if the business activity necessitates it (such as Madeleine's livestock activity that takes time to realize a profit).

MADELINE DURING HER LOAN GROUP MEETING

Additionally, every client is provided a savings account and encouraged to save for future needs and is also able to withdraw funds whenever necessary. While clients meet with their loan officer in groups with other borrowers, the liability for the loans is completely individual, with groups serving solely as a platform to reimburse, save, and access Entrepreneur du Monde's 34 different training modules. These modules range from financial literacy to business skills. Groups can participate in trainings on subjects like strategies for increasing profit margins, starting a new business, and overcoming volatility in energy access and costs.

In many countries, local regulations make it very difficult for socially-minded financial service providers to offer more than just microloans, even if they would like to expand services to their clients. The methodology Entrepreneurs du Monde is expanding is both expensive and labor intensive, and Entrepreneurs du Monde in Burkina Faso is still working to scale to a size that can show that its model can break even despite high operating costs and logistical challenges (plus mandated caps on the fee they can charge for their services which is lower than surrounding regions). The program has only just begun to reach into rural areas outside the capital which will prove even more difficult to serve in a cost-effective way.

However, if more microfinance institutions can expand access to more diverse and tailored services, the benefits can be great. Hopefully more countries can increase incentives to microfinance institutions to encourage them to expand the services they offer. Whole Planet Foundation has supported Entrepreneurs du Monde affiliates in Cambodia, Togo, Ghana, India and the Philippines.

Chapter 9

Interest Rates and our Microfinance Programs

By Philip Sansone and Jessica Villanueva

Whole Planet Foundation provides grants and interest free loans to our microfinance partners and does not set the interest rates of our partners. Interest Rates charged by Whole Planet Foundation's microfinance partners are impacted by a number of factors and vary by country.

We work only with microfinance partners, or MFIs, that have agreed to keep the interest as low as possible. Even though interest rates are kept as low as possible, the interest has to cover inflation, cost of borrowing capital, MFI overhead and other associated health, savings, insurance and education services, (when these services are offered). A modest profit is necessary to stay in business and continue to offer financial services to the very poor and to continue to grow (or, in the case of a nonprofit, a year end "net asset", which is same thing although generally nontaxable).

Sometimes interest rates seem very high by Western standards, but the highest rates inevitably come from moneylenders who are traditionally the only ones willing to lend to the poor. Usually, the higher the risk, the higher the interest rate – and that can be substantial – but the microentrepreneurs are very good at repaying loans that are appropriately sized for their capacity. Worldwide, 96% pay their loans.

Whole Planet Foundation partners are committed to pricing transparency that clearly informs clients of the cost of the loan. The borrowers, thus, make informed decisions to invest capital and grow their businesses. Through microloans, borrowers can grow their businesses and the earnings from these new revenues easily surpass the interest paid on the loans.

Interest rates are determined by five main factors:

1. Rate of inflation in the country:
   - Double digit and even triple digit inflation are not uncommon in developing countries. Interest rates must cover inflation. Recently Venezuela had inflation of over 1 million percent, Zimbabwe 98% and Argentina 56%.

2. Cost of capital (COC):
   - This refers to cash in the capital market (banks etc.) that MFIs use to relend to poor borrowers. Think of COC as the wholesale price of the product, which is money that is then lent in loans. Hundreds of billions of dollars will be needed to fund the billions of potential poor borrowers.
   - Cost of capital (COC) is often well into double digits 15-20% in developing countries. Interest rates must cover inflation + cost of capital (COC usually does cover some of the inflation, but often not all.)

3. MFIs overhead expenses or the cost of providing the loan is very high:
   - Most successful operations usually visit borrowers 25-50 times a year at locations near the borrower's homes which takes an

army of field loan officers, motorcycles and other support.
- o Traditional banks can't do this. Interest rates must cover inflation + cost of capital + MFI overhead.

4. Other associated services, such as health, savings, insurance and education services that must be paid for from interest collected or "fees" charged to the microentrepreneur:
- o Some MFIs believe it is imperative that they extend other crucial services to the poor along with the loan. These can include:
    - Health exams and other medical services such as family planning and reproductive and parenting education
    - Business advice and education or training
    - Marketing advice and assistance for their crops or products
    - Mandatory savings (often cited as necessary to escape poverty)
    - Health and/or life insurance.

5. Profits or excess capital; i.e. net assets at year-end:
- o Profit, or for the non-profit "excess capital/net assets" is important to keep the MFI operating so that it can continue working to help the poor. Either way, the MFI must end up the year profitable or face going out of business.

In sum: interest must be enough to cover:

- o Inflation
- o Cost of capital

- Overhead expenses
- Other services
- And to create a profit or excess capital at year's end

Our microfinance partners are charged with trying to provide interest rates as low as possible while navigating the complexities of lending to the poor. Whole Planet Foundation works to identify and fund MFIs who have agreed to keep their interest rates low while providing the highest level of service to their clients.

Part II:

MFIS: SPOTLIGHT ON SOME OUR MICROFINANCE INSTITUTION PARTNERS

Latin America

Chapter 1

Fundación Paraguaya: Microfinance in Paraguay

By Roxana Newton

In 2015, our microfinance partner in Paraguay, Fundación Paraguaya, won Whole Planet Foundation's microfinance organization of the year. When I had the opportunity to visit them, I was impressed not only by the lending program, but also its agricultural education program.

Agricultural Education

Fundación Paraguaya has three schools: San Pedro, San Francisco and Bethlehem. We visited the school in San Pedro primarily because Fundación Paraguaya decided to use the prize money they received from Whole Planet Foundation to build a dining hall and kitchen for their students.

Each school's program is different; however, the objective is the same: to provide an opportunity to low-income students to acquire the skills and knowledge to overcome poverty. In San Pedro, the students' ages range from 15-19, and for the most part all are extremely poor. Each student pays $10 a month to attend school – this includes room and board. Most of the students go for months without visiting their parents because bus passes are too expensive for them.

The San Pedro program is a two-year program and focuses on business and agricultural skills. They do have formal classes, but much of the work is practical. Their model is "learning by doing, selling and winning." Students participate in the entire production cycle and marketing and selling of a product. They learn how to farm, take care of livestock, and how to package & market the goods they produce and raise.

A Pipeline to Business Success

With the produce and chickens they raise, the students work with instructors to establish a client base in the community, both individuals and commercial. The school uses the profits to cover its operational expenses. At the time of the visit, the San Pedro School was about 30% self-sufficient, but they hope to reach 100% in a few years. This would mean the students and teachers would have to sell at least $140,000 in products annually.

THE GARDEN AT THE SAN PEDRO SCHOOL. THEY ARE IN THE MIDST OF EXPANDING IT IN ORDER TO PRODUCE MORE CROPS.

At the end of the program, each student must present and defend a business plan. The goal is that each student can graduate from the program and start his or her own business. Furthermore, they receive the opportunity to apply for a loan through Fundación Paraguaya's microlending program.

Chapter 2

Funding Opportunities with Friendship Bridge in Guatemala

By Friendship Bridge & Whole Planet Foundation

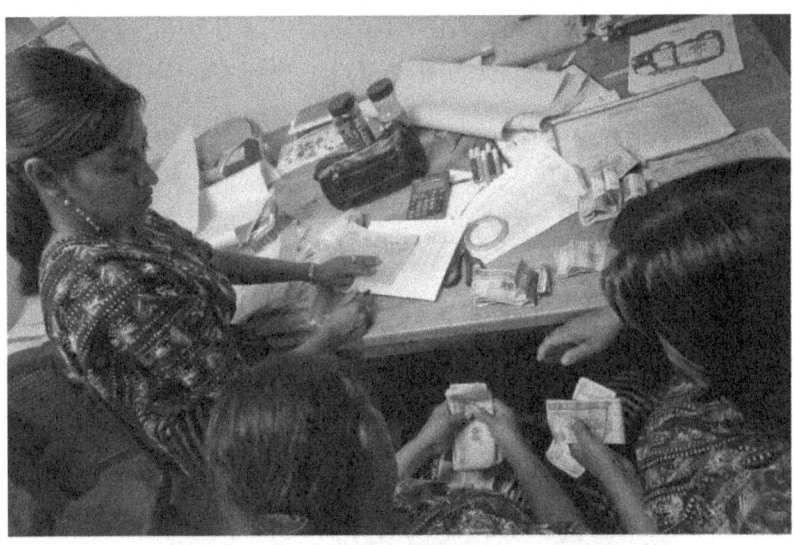

FRIENDSHIP BRIDGE CLIENTS PAY INSTALLMENTS ON THEIR LOANS IN SOLOLÁ, GUATEMALA. ONCE A MONTH THE WOMEN MEET WITH THEIR TRUST BANK, PAY INSTALLMENTS ON THEIR LOANS, AND RECEIVE NON-FORMAL EDUCATION WHICH IS A CORNERSTONE OF FRIENDSHIP BRIDGE'S MICROCREDIT PLUS PROGRAM.

Over the course of the next three years, Friendship Bridge will receive $300,000 from Whole Planet Foundation to support its new branch in Huehuetenango. There is an unmet need in the country, especially in the most rural areas that other microfinance organizations have steered away from due to the higher operating costs required to reach these communities. Providing services to these women requires additional expenses due to the logistics of attending to these communities that limits the funds available to provide loan capital.

WPF support will enable Friendship Bridge to lessen that gap and help meet the needs of women in difficult to reach, rural areas. Over the course of the project, Friendship Bridge plans to serve more than 2,300 women in the region.

Serving the Underserved

In Guatemala, there are a significant number of microfinance institutions (banks, NGOs, credit unions etc.) who provide access to finance to the country's poor. However, the majority of these institutions serve primarily urban and peri-urban communities, and many of these communities are in fact saturated with microfinance institutions and their advertising programs. Due to the visibility and prevalence of these institutions, over- indebtedness can be a significant issue if an organization does not implement certain safeguards (i.e. credit checks, limiting the number of loans a potential client can have, pre-credit training, etc.).

Friendship Bridge protects its clients against over-indebtedness through thorough credit analysis and background checks, ongoing monitoring of clients' credit scores, and providing training modules on how to borrow responsibly.

In rural areas, access to finance remains a challenge. Rural areas remain harder to serve in terms of cost and logistics. Despite the inherent challenges, Friendship Bridge is committed to providing socially responsible finance and expanding its reach into rural areas.

Creating Opportunities for Women

Friendship Bridge's mission is to create opportunities that empower Guatemalan women to build a better life.

FRIENDSHIP BRIDGE CLIENT, MARIA, WEAVES ON A BACKSTRAP LOOM IN THE SUCHITEPÉQUEZ DEPARTMENT OF GUATEMALA. FRIENDSHIP BRIDGE SERVES WOMEN OF RURAL GUATEMALA ACROSS 12 DEPARTMENTS THROUGH SEVEN BRANCHES AND TWO SATELLITE OFFICES.

Friendship Bridge began its work in Vietnam by providing medical education and shipping of medical supplies to impoverished populations in war-ravaged areas. In 1994, after deciding to focus on a more sustainable solution to poverty reduction, Friendship Bridge shifted its focus from medical supplies to microcredit. In 1998, Friendship Bridge expanded its work to Guatemala, another country impacted by war and extreme poverty, by offering limited opportunities to women. Friendship Bridge shifted out of Vietnam and began focusing solely on a Microcredit Plus program in Guatemala. By 2003, almost 3,000 clients were borrowing from Friendship Bridge in Guatemala. By 2006 the number tripled to 9,000 clients, and by the end of 2016 they had reached more than 29,000 women through their Microcredit Plus program.

A FRIENDSHIP BRIDGE CLIENT POSES WITH A BOWL OF TORTILLAS THAT SHE WILL SELL IN HER COMMUNITY

Friendship Bridge's Microcredit Plus program provides loans for women to support their businesses and education to strengthen and train their clients on diverse topics including financial literacy, women's rights and health.

On average, a Friendship Bridge client is a 38-year-old woman, has had approximately three years of formal education, participates in the informal economy, and cannot read or write. The majority of clients have limited fluency in Guatemala's official language, Spanish, and instead speak one of 24 indigenous languages. The average client's household earns between $1.11 and $4.49 a day, which may be categorized as "poor, extremely vulnerable or vulnerable" according to the Grameen Foundation's PPI.

Each client participates in a Trust Bank Loan, which is Friendship Bridge's primary loan product. The average new Trust Bank loan is $318 and is repaid over a 12-month period. Over the years, Friendship Bridge has introduced new loan products tailored to meet its clients' needs. Clients with a strong repayment and attendance history are eligible to access these additional products:

1. *CrediSalud* enables clients to purchase efficient, clean-burning stoves that replace open fires in the home. This product saves clients an average of $37 per month in fuel and reduces health conditions associated with smoke inhalation.
2. *Crediescolar* provides for the costs associated with school enrollment, such as uniforms and school fees. In 2015, 86% of clients used the loan to continue their children's education, and 14% used it to enroll a student for the first time.
3. *Rapidito* is a small, fast loan product that allows clients to cover unexpected expenses or to take advantage of business opportunities. Rapidito often

enables clients to purchase or produce additional inventory for holidays when the opportunity for commerce is high.

4. *Paralelo* provides additional capital for clients who have good credit history and business potential in order to further grow their businesses.

"Microcredit Plus"

Friendship Bridge continues to innovate and adapt its services and loan products to meet the needs of microcredit clients. Its Microcredit Plus program combines small business loans with basic non-formal education in tandem with opportunities for more advanced trainings and mentorship tailored to clients' individual experiences and aptitudes. Beyond the non-formal education that clients receive once a month at their trust bank meeting, clients also receive five plus services at no additional cost: advanced education, mentorship, artisan market access, health services, and agriculture training.

A GROUP OF WOMEN WHO ARE PART OF THE SAME TRUST BANK LEARN ABOUT FAMILY PLANNING DURING A NON-FORMAL EDUCATION SESSION

In 2015, Friendship Bridge introduced a mentorship program as well as its Artisan Market Access Program. The artisan program provides the opportunity for existing clients to receive technical and business skills to access new local, national and international markets. As part of this program, Friendship Bridge has created an online store as a means to assist their clients in reaching new markets. Friendship Bridge has even worked with these clients to refine their products to ensure they are market ready.

In 2015, Friendship Bridge introduced its women's preventive health program, Salud para la Vida. It is designed to specifically counter the healthcare challenges that rural, indigenous women face in Guatemala. This service provides the opportunity for clients to receive free or low-cost preventive health services and screenings in their communities.

Chapter 3

Assessing Poverty with a Stoplight
By Roxana Newton

THE POVERTY STOPLIGHT TOOL PUTS POVERTY ASSESSMENT IN THE HANDS
OF THE PEOPLE EXPERIENCING POVERTY.

Whole Planet Foundation supports microfinance institutions (MFIs) serving vulnerable communities and promoting financial inclusion throughout these communities throughout the world.

You may be wondering: how do WPF partners identify their target clients and communities? How do they measure their impact on these communities and individual families?

Many of our partners use poverty measurement tools to assess if they are reaching their target and determine what percentage of their client base are 'poor'. The Ford

Foundation, CGAP, the EU and the Social Performance Task Force compiled a report in 2010 Poverty Targeting and Measurement Tools in Microfinance. The report describes two tools constructed and the feedback received on those tools.

A MICROCREDIT CLIENT. PHOTO COURTESY OF FUNDACIÓN PARAGUAYA

The most common survey is the PPI or the Progress out of Poverty tool designed by Grameen. The other example is the Poverty Assessment Tool (PAT) designed by USAID. The PPI measures 'the estimation of a group's poverty rate at a point in time and an estimation of changes in a group's poverty rate between two points in time'. The PAT measures 'an estimation of the poverty outreach of an organization, as a percentage of its client population that is below one or more poverty lines'.

Of the partners using a poverty measurement tool, many are using the PPI or a version of this tool. WPF's partner in Paraguay, Fundación Paraguaya, has created its own tool – the Poverty Stoplight.

A Solution for Assessing Poverty

Fundación Paraguaya realized that many of their clients were still continuing to struggle with poverty-related challenges despite access to microfinance and increase in family income. Fundación Paraguaya decided to build its own tool that would allow the client to assess their own status and develop an action plan on how to improve their own family's situation.

A MICROCREDIT CLIENT. PHOTO COURTESY OF FUNDACIÓN PARAGUAYA

The Poverty Stoplight is both a metric and a methodology that enables families to assess their level of poverty and to implement individual, personalized strategies to overcome their families' specific challenges. It defines what it means *not* to be poor across six dimensions: income & employment, health & environment, housing &

infrastructure, education & culture, organization & participation, and interiority & motivation.

The six dimensions are divided into 50 indicators and each indicator is represented by three images. Each participant self-evaluates her/himself according to the picture: extreme poverty (red), poverty (yellow) and non-poverty (green). The indicators are both internal (income) and external (poor roads).

Participants are able to complete the evaluation on a mobile phone, tablet or computer. They also receive their own pamphlet with all 50 indicators and stickers (red, yellow and green) that the participants are able to update as they move forward on their path out of poverty. After the evaluation, the results allow the participant to visualize and understand their strength and weakness and helps them create and focus on concrete actions and setting priorities.

Observing the Poverty Stoplight in Action

I recently had the opportunity to visit Fundación Paraguaya. During my visit, a client let me watch her as she completed the Poverty Stoplight self-evaluation. She has been a client of Fundación Paraguaya for many years and has a stable business, income and receives additional support from her husband that works in the remote El Chaco region. Many of her red indicators were external factors including lack of garbage collection and poor streets. When I asked Fundacíon Paraguaya what can be done in this situation, the loan officer responded that Fundación Paraguaya can be a resource and help them identify what can be done.

Another group I met with had already been to the city to try to address a very poor road in their community (that was further damaged by the 2016 floods). Unfortunately, they did not have much luck with their municipality, but they did come together as a group to do bake sales to raise funds to fix the road themselves.

Another poverty indicator is the state of the family's bathroom (latrine, inside bathroom etc.) Fixing this indicator can be expensive, so Fundación Paraguaya has implemented a series of 'contests' under the assumption that peer support and motivation can lead to a significant (positive) change.

One of these contests is the "My Bathroom, My Kitchen, My Pride" contest. Banco communales choose the woman with the worst bathroom and together as a group they raise money and fix the bathroom. What Fundación Paraguaya realized, was that this started a chain reaction and over time the groups would begin working on other member's bathrooms. With a small investment (prize money) the overall impact of these types of contests are enormous.

The Poverty Stoplight around the Globe
Fundación Paraguaya also uses the tool within its own organizations and works with other private organizations to adopt the tool and implement it internally. As of 2016, 86 other companies in Paraguay have used the Poverty Stoplight internally, with their staff. On an international level, organizations in more than 20 countries ranging from the United States to Pakistan to Vietnam have or are implementing the Poverty Stoplight tool as of the writing of this post. Each of the indicators are adapted to

the specific country context because what it means to be poor in Mexico is not the same as being poor in Tanzania.

To read more about the Poverty Spotlight, visit https://www.povertystoplight.org/en/.

Chapter 4

Human Resilience, Microfinance, and the Evolution of Potatoes

By J.P. Kloninger

JP ON A 2019 MONITORING AND EVALUATION TRIP TO BOLIVIA. WPF'S FIELD STAFF TRAVEL TO VISIT OUR CURRENT MICROFINANCE PARTNERS AND IDENTIFY NEW PARTNERS IN OUR PROGRAM COUNTRIES

These unprecedented times during the beginnings of this global COVID-19 pandemic bring to mind a movie line by Gunnery Sergeant Thomas Highway, played by Clint Eastwood in Heartbreak Ridge: "Improvise, Adapt, and Overcome."

Those three words have become something of a mantra to me. The approach they suggest, in addition to appearing especially relevant these days, are in line with the resourcefulness, adaptability, and resilience of the people we meet and learn from in our travels for Whole Planet Foundation. Among them are not only the microentrepreneurs who constantly amaze us with the value they are able to create with just a small amount of credit, but also the staff of the microfinance institutions we actively work with in 77 countries around the world.

Resourcefulness in Bolivia

One of those 77 countries is Bolivia, where Whole Planet Foundation funds a microfinance organization called Sembrar Sartawi. Sartawi means "lift oneself" in the language of the Aymara, a culture native to the Altiplano, an expansive plateau in the highlands of the South American Andes mountain range. In these regions there are over 200,000 producers in farming and related activities.

With nearly 30,000 clients and growing, Sembrar Sartawi offers innovative products and services to rural agricultural regions of Bolivia. In these regions there are over 200,000 producers in farming and related activities, many of whom could benefit from Sembrar Sartawi's offerings. With those producers in mind, Sembrar Sartawi offers both "solidarity group" credit and individual loans; an "agro-climactic" insurance product for clients who are exposed to the risks and uncertainties in productive agriculture, especially in light of climate change patterns; and on-staff technical experts such as agronomists and veterinarians, who offer their know-how to clients receiving credit from Sembrar Sartawi.

Whole Planet Foundation provides capital for microcredit products designed to provide business-enhancing opportunities for solidarity group borrowers of bancas comunales in Sembrar Sartawi's Potosí branch, located in the southern Altiplano, about 340 miles south of the country's administrative capital, La Paz.

SEMBRAR SARTAWI'S POTOSÍ BRANCH IS LOCATED IN THE SOUTHERN ALTIPLANO ABOUT 340 MILES SOUTH OF THE COUNTRY'S ADMINISTRATIVE CAPITAL, LA PAZ

Sembrar Sartawi's solidarity groups are comprised mainly of women living in rural Bolivia. While the members of these solidarity groups (i.e. banca comunales) run a wide variety of small businesses, many of them grow potatoes both for self-subsistence and sale at local markets. This is a logical connection considering that the potato has been central to the region's economy and livelihood since this root vegetable was first domesticated around 10,000 years ago, in what is now southern Peru and northwestern Bolivia.

Chuños and Tuntas: Innovation at Work

During a field visit that WPF's Global Director, Daniel, and I made to Bolivia in early 2019, we learned volumes about recent changes in the country's microfinance regulatory environment, and the effects they have had on stakeholders in that sector. More unexpectedly, we learned a lot about potatoes! Simply by being in Bolivia, one is immersed in potatoes during meals and conversations about their cultivation, history, and significance in this part of the world.

Over 4,000 varieties of native potatoes have been identified in the Andean highlands. Learning about "chuños" and "tuntas" proved particularly interesting. These are potatoes which have been dehydrated following a precise sequence including freezing them and exposing them to the sun, mainly to preserve them for extended periods of time but also for transformed and improved nutritional properties, taste, and a range of cooking possibilities.

A couple of days into our trip to Bolivia, my interest in the region's potato lore was piqued when towards the end of a microcredit borrowers' group meeting just outside of La Paz, one of the elder "cholitas" -a Bolivian indigenous woman - (bowler hat, pleated skirt, and all!) started speaking directly to us in what must have been either Quechua or Aymara. All I could really tell was that she was talking to us about potatoes, and she mentioned chuños, which we had just learned about the day before while having lunch in El Alto, a large open-air market where many microloan recipients sell their wares.

EL ALTO, A LARGE OPEN-AIR MARKET, OVERLOOKS THE CITY

While I did not understand the woman's exact words, I will always remember her and that moment – it was one of the highlights of a trip that gave me a heightened appreciation for human innovation and resilience. There are few places I have traveled which more clearly demonstrated to me the human ability to "improvise, adapt, and overcome."

Thousands of years ago, with very challenging conditions for year-round subsistence agriculture, the inhabitants of the Andean highlands developed techniques to transform the potato into chuño (black sun-dried potato) and tunta (white sun-dried potato), giving them the ability to store their food for longer periods of time.

The potato has since spread around the world and become an important staple crop in many countries, for diverse cultures who prepare them in countless healthy and tasty ways. A simple tuber from the Andes has evolved into a global nutritional powerhouse.

Improvise, Adapt, and Overcome

Not unlike the Andean ancestors that developed the chuño and the tunta to survive and to flourish in a harsh environment, I believe that COVID-19 will soon be sustainably controlled. We will develop new ways to engage in commerce — such as our microfinance partners are already doing around the world — and new technologies will emerge in all impacted sectors, along with wiser ways of thinking about nature, our existence within it, and our co-existence. I have no doubt we will "improvise, adapt, and overcome", and as our Bolivian partner Sembrar Sartawi's name suggests, we will yet again "lift ourselves" to a new place and to better lives.

Chapter 5

Aflore and WPF Help Small Businesses Blossom in Colombia

By J.P. Kloninger

Whole Planet Foundation was created to support communities worldwide where Whole Foods Market sources products. Flowers for Whole Foods Market stores across the US, Canada, and the UK, along with many other products, are sourced in large quantities from Colombia — so while it's perhaps a bit of a happy coincidence, it seems quite fitting that Whole Planet Foundation's newest microfinance partner in Colombia is called Aflore, the name of which comes from the Spanish word flor, for 'flower.'

Aflore comes from the infinitive "aflorar", which means "to surface, to appear," as in flowers surfacing or appearing, and Aflore is certainly doing that – helping thousands of microentrepreneurs to 'blossom' with their own businesses. Not only is Aflore providing microloans to people with little or no access to conventional banks in Colombia, but through a very innovative business model and smartphone technology, they are also empowering thousands of "Informal Advisors" ("IAs", and in Spanish, "consejeras") to reach out to their own social networks and offer loans that catalyze borrowers' small businesses, thus helping the economic stability of their families and surrounding communities.

INFORMAL ADVISOR (IA) ADRIANA IN BARRIO SAN PABLO, MEDELLÍN. SHE IS SHOWING THE FREE SMARTPHONE AFLORE GAVE HER, WHICH USES THE INNOVATIVE MI AFLORE APP

Informal Advisors Create Networks for Success

Via its consejeras, Aflore identifies the trust and relationships which already exist within communities and formalizes them to enable loan agreements. Aflore leans on a direct sales model and finds leaders in the community (for example, residents who have already been engaging their neighbors in home-sales of merchandise) who are then trained in Aflore's processes, procedures, and tools to bring financial products to the underbanked.

I visited Aflore at their head office in Bogotá in 2018, and then flew over to Medellín, where they opened a new branch office less than a year ago. After a favorable review of the organization's structure, strategy, systems, and in-field operations, we decided to support the Medellín project to allow Aflore to scale significantly in this new region of Colombia, and to further prove their lending concept which is already successful in Bogotá. With Whole Planet's funding, Aflore aims to reach over 1500 new microentrepreneurs in Medellín over the next three years.

To me, Aflore's model stands out as being quite unique compared to many of Whole Planet Foundation's traditional microfinance partners, whose loan officers' many responsibilities include identifying new loan recipients, conducting borrower meetings periodically (often weekly or biweekly), ensuring timely repayments, and even transporting cash to and from borrowers. In contrast, Aflore's outreach strategy is similar to that of a direct-sales company – IAs are recruited, trained and incentivized to leverage their community networks, focusing mainly on identifying new clients (loan origination). Aflore then manages the network, the loans, and related analysis and risk-mitigation. This model is enabled with innovative, user-friendly technology such as the Mi Aflore phone app that is used to collect borrower information, submit loan applications, manage loan portfolios, communicate with peers and financial and tech support, etc.

While ultimately the loan agreements are directly between the borrower-entrepreneur and Aflore, the IA has an incentive to find good prospective clients since she receives a commission upon securing a loan, gains points (called Florines) that she can exchange for cash or prizes such as home appliances, becomes part of a supportive peer community (also via the Mi Aflore app), and gains the satisfaction of introducing a very valuable service in her own neighborhood. Further, a consejera can also apply for and obtain a loan from Aflore herself. Consejeras also help Aflore maintain a high, on-time repayment rate, being reminded by the app a few days in advance of when her clients' loan installments are due.

As our global communities evolve and as the world's poor face new challenges but also new opportunities to lift themselves out of poverty, it is very encouraging to see microfinance evolving as well, through fresh, dynamic ideas which organizations such as Aflore in Colombia bring to market.

Asia-Pacific Region

Chapter 1

KOMIDA'S Social Performance Management Journey
By Claire Kelly

A KOMIDA GROUP MEETING

As part of Whole Planet Foundation's annual due diligence visits to our microfinance partners around the globe, we observe the presence or absence of "responsible finance indicators" which shed light on how our partners are serving the world's poorest people. Many of our microfinance partners use or develop strategies to inform their work, ensuring they are reaching their target populations with the services they need most.

WPF's Indonesian microfinance partner, KOMIDA, was recently highlighted in a case study which was featured on Microfinance Gateway for their work in the field of Social Performance Management. As it pertains to microfinance institutions (MFIs), CGAP defines Social Performance Management as: *"...the systems that organizations use to achieve their stated social goals and put customers at the center of strategy andoperations. A provider's social performance refers to its effectiveness in achieving its stated social goals and creating value for clients."*

KOMIDA operates out of 230 branches in 11 provinces: Aceh, Banten, West Java, Central Java, East Java, Yogyakarta, West Nusa Tenggara, East Nusa Tenggara, South Sulawesi, West Sulawesi, and South Kalimantan. As of June 2018, KOMIDA had over 487,226 active borrowers and a loan portfolio of over $60 million. This makes KOMIDA the second largest microfinance institution in Indonesia.

A Focus on the Poorest Populations

KOMIDA began offering microfinance services in 2005 to help tsunami victims in Aceh, Indonesia. The organization has steadily built on this social focus. When they first began their work, KOMIDA used a questionnaire called the Cashpor Housing Index (CHI) to help them appropriately target clients. In mid-2017, KOMIDA reviewed the CHI, and after discussion by management, KOMIDA decided to change some CHI indicators in order to adjust to the condition of Indonesian society. Their new system is now called the KHI (KOMIDA House Index), and it is currently under a review process in new branches as of the writing of this post.

The KHI requires field staff to ask clients about the height of their home's walls and materials of their home's construction. The KHI is based on the fact that poor people tend to spend their money first on basic needs, then social obligations, and finally on housing. Therefore, the KHI reveals not only the quality of the house but is also an indicator of the wealth of the household itself.

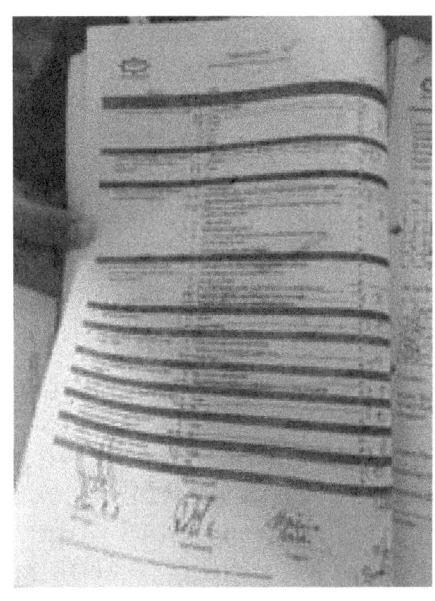

THE POVERTY PROBABILITY INDEX (PPI) AT KOMIDA

In addition to the KHI, the Poverty Probability Index (PPI) is another tool that can be used to identify and measure the poverty level of incoming clients. The PPI asks a series of questions about the type of housing, assets of the household and education of the family. Each answer has a score. These are totaled together. The score is then coded to a look-up table where it can be matched with a percentage indicating the likelihood that this household is living below the poverty line. The PPI is updated and modified for each country to be aligned with the specific context, and as of June 2018, KOMIDA served 6.5% clients living below the National Poverty Line of Indonesia. 9.8% of their clients are living below $1.25 USD/day and 64.8% of clients are living on less than $2.50 USD/day.

From 2009 until 2018, KOMIDA adapted the PPI and also refined their mission statement. The management team demonstrates full commitment to achieving their social goals, especially at a time where different forms of lending could be more commercially viable for the organization. KOMIDA's use of the PPI is a critical part of this mission. Their use of the Index ensures they cater to women below the poverty level to create programs and products that make a difference in improving their livelihoods.

Social Performance Management

In 2015, KOMIDA created a Social Performance Management (SPM) team, including a SPM champion on their board of directors. Another focus during this period was implementing client protection principles. These steps included developing an SMS number for customer feedback, responsible pricing, feedback surveys for product development and a focus on increasing the staff retention rate. KOMIDA also conducts client satisfaction surveys in order to get information and feedback from clients about their preferences and complaints so they can better meet their clients' needs. This is done as part of KOMIDA's commitment to the SMART Campaign's 7 Client Protection Principles.

Here is a snapshot of some of the Social Indicators which KOMIDA follows:

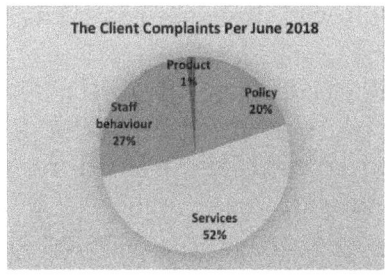

The Client Complaints Per June 2018

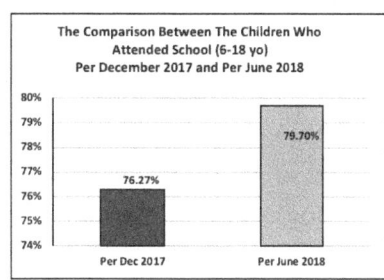

The Comparison Between The Children Who Attended School (6-18 yo) Per December 2017 and Per June 2018

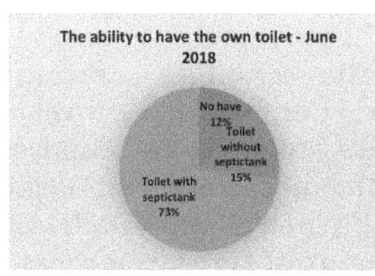

The ability to have the own toilet - June 2018

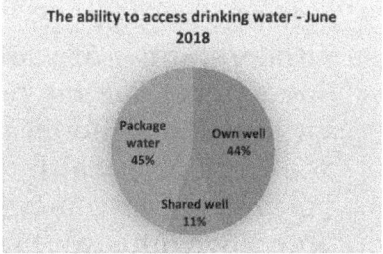

The ability to access drinking water - June 2018

In 2015, KOMIDA engaged with Opportunity International for technical assistance to evaluate KOMIDA's social performance using a social audit tool. As Annadanam explains in a CGAP case study, there were four main reasons why KOMIDA decided to implement the Universal Standards for SPM:

1. To hold itself accountable to its social mission. KOMIDA genuinely wanted to create positive effects in clients' lives, and it recognized that good SPM would help it to achieve its goals.

2. To understand what outcomes KOMIDA's clients had actually been experiencing. The board, management, and staff felt that there was no proof beyond the anecdotal evidence that they had gathered about how KOMIDA's services were affecting clients' lives. KOMIDA knew that implementing SPM would help the team get a true

understanding of how clients' lives were changing, for better or worse.

3. To understand to what extent KOMIDA was complying with the global standards of SPM. This is a topic of increasing relevance to funders and regulators around the world.

4. To respond to social investors' requests for SPM data that went beyond the PPI. While the PPI is a great tool to understand the poverty levels of clients, other SPM data are required to understand all of the changes (meaning, outcomes) taking place. For instance, investors wanted additional data related to children's education, health outcomes, and household income improvements. Furthermore, KOMIDA did not have data on the quality of services, except for the proxy of client exit rate, and it lacked data on client satisfaction and client complaint resolution.

After receiving the scores and analysis from the audit process, KOMIDA engaged their team across all departments and modified the organization's strategy by creating an action plan. This was an iterative process taking place from 2015-2016. KOMIDA paid all the costs of implementing the action plan and acted carefully to make it as affordable as possible. KOMIDA now tracks the number of MFIs who operate in all regions and they form expansion plans which prioritize moving into less penetrated areas. This addresses the risk of client over-indebtedness (Annadanam, 11).

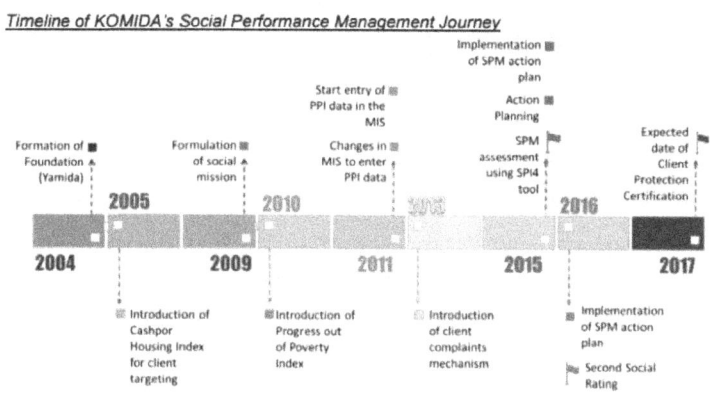

Timeline of KOMIDA's Social Performance Management Journey

FIGURE 4(ANNADANAM, 5)

Empowering Staff Members

Another example of aligning social performance metrics with operating procedures is the Staff Appraisal Form. KOMIDA includes six points of social performance for evaluating the staff's competency. Those staff's competencies are:

1. Their concern for environmental issues
2. Alignment with organization, vision, mission, and values
3. Customer service
4. Ethical behavior
5. Adherence to organizational policies
6. Attitude toward clients and co-workers.

Through ongoing appraisals and training of their staff, KOMIDA hopes that all staff members have the social performance competencies for offering the best services to clients. These targets are checked using KOMIDA's internal audit department.

Conclusions

The SPM initiative was led by KOMIDA's Founder and Managing director, Mr. Slamet Riyadi, who explains,

"KOMIDA was established not only to provide access to credit for poor families in Indonesia, but also to use the credit program to bring positive change for them. This thinking differentiates KOMIDA from many other financial institutions in Indonesia that focus on financial performance rather than on client outcomes or their well-being. KOMIDA wanted to change such stereotypes and bring the focus back on poor households. KOMIDA shall ensure that any loans given to the client households should help them achieve a better life. Social performance management (SPM) helped KOMIDA in this aspect as it provided a framework that influenced the development of clear social goals and objectives. The data from SPM also helped KOMIDA in analyzing if the social goals (especially client well-being) were met or not."

Whole Planet Foundation doesn't require that our partners administer any one specific tool. Rather, as part of our field team's annual monitoring visits, we observe the presence or absence of specific "responsible finance indicators" that pull from each of these industry tools.

As you can see from KOMIDA's history, there are many tools that MFIs can use to implement responsible finance. These include the Poverty Probability Index, the CASHPOR Housing Index, the SMART Campaign, the SPI4, and others. Some of our smaller partners don't have the capacity for working with consultants in such an all-inclusive way as KOMIDA did. However, the thoughtful, comprehensive way that KOMIDA has used to integrate SPM into their social mission, day-to-day operations AND management decisions is a strong example for other microfinance institutions to follow.

Chapter 2

Microfinance vs. Informal Finance: A Fair Comparison?
By Claire Kelly

STAFF OF BRAC MYANMAR IN FRONT OF A BRANCH OFFICE

If microfinance is so effective, then why hasn't the industry put informal moneylenders out of business?

This is the question that a recent paper, *"Microfinance for poverty alleviation: Do transnational initiatives overlook fundamental questions of competition and intermediation?"* in Transnational Corporations and the accompanying blog set out to find the answer to. Frithjof, Ardisa and Ardisa, the authors of the original paper, use the approach of examining other market players in Indonesia, rather than a specific microfinance program, to get their insights.

To take the conversation forward, I wanted to point out a few strategies and programs that Whole Planet Foundation and our microfinance partners implement to address these concerns.

Informal and Formal Finance Structures

The authors of the study referenced above identify the existence of different types of informal finance and explore how these various informal finance players thrive in Indonesia despite the prevalence of low-cost microcredit. They suggest that some elements of informal finance should be more widely integrated into formal finance.

Most people are familiar with the idea of a loan shark. However, another less well-known actor in the informal finance space is an "intermediary." This would essentially be a small business owner who borrows an amount in excess of what s/he needs for her own business from a microfinance program. Then she lends out the extra money to others in the community. The researchers found that this can occur when the poorest/smallest entrepreneurs are unable to access the credit directly from the microfinance institution (MFI), potentially because they lack the necessary documents. And the process is facilitated by MFI credit officers, who are often not well trained or are incentivized to provide loans only to non-risky clients they are confident will repay.

Choosing Our Partners

I see how this situation could occur at an MFI with no social mission, weak management and incentives that do not align with a stated mission. However, all of Whole Planet Foundation's microfinance partners are specifically chosen because of their pro-poor methodology, which includes offering products that are inclusive and accessible to the poorest entrepreneurs. Significantly, our due diligence analysis of our partners does not just include the MFI's mission statement, but an analysis of how the MFI's loan processes, HR incentives and overall management align.

It takes a strong social mission, as well as policies that reinforce this mission, management and staff trained to implement to avoid a situation where informal financial intermediaries might flourish among the MFI's clients.

Some of the questions WPF asks during our team's due diligence visits include:

- What is the system to identify low income community members to join the microfinance program?
- Do field staff visit the home and/or business of a client to determine repayment capacity and business plan?
- Do field staff verify that the MFI loan has been used for the stated purpose?
- Is there an internal audit department & does it report directly to the board?
- Are field offers incentivized for portfolio value & repayment rate alone?
- How does field officer salary compare to average GDP?

STAFF AT THE DAIK-U BAGO BRANCH OF BRAC MYANMAR

Systems for Success

In Indonesia, WPF partners with KOMIDA. This social MFI has done significant work on their social performance management (SPM), specifically integrating social performance targets across all of their departments and aligning loan products, operations, and services with their social mission. For example, KOMIDA is targeting clients who don't have access to financial services, supporting their clients to have financial literacy through the financial education, and training staff about social performance competency. One specific strategy to prevent field staff from becoming informal finance intermediaries is to evaluate staff attitude in line with the organizational vision, mission and values rather than their portfolio performance alone.

Another excellent example of a social MFI with strong management is Whole Planet Foundation's microfinance partner BRAC Myanmar Microfinance Company Limited. The organization leverages the expertise from their largest operation in Bangladesh to immediately scale up credit programs in a systematic and controlled manner. This means programs such as internal audits, human resources and a network of regional management are in place from the beginning. As the organization develops, these roles are increasingly transferred back to host country nationals who have been trained. The well detailed loan procedures and trained field staff at a partner like BRAC Myanmar Microfinance Company Limited would make it very difficult for an informal financial intermediary to operate.

Trade-Financiers

In addition to loan sharks and informal finance intermediaries, a trade-financier is another actor who operates in the informal finance sector. These are typically small businesses who might provide free seeds and fertilizers at the beginning of a season, and their customer must repay at harvest by agreeing to sell a certain amount of their harvest back to the trade-financer (typically below market price). Given that these arrangements are usually much more expensive than a microloan for the clients, the authors of the study try to understand – why are the trade-financiers still in business?

Their conclusion is that the trade-financiers are providing valuable services beyond that of a typical MFI

– services like the farm inputs and guaranteed markets. On the other hand, the clients likely do not fully understand how much they are paying for the services of the trade financier since the arrangement is not presented in a clear way, stating the loan amount plus interest amount. The researchers' solutions to these problems are twofold: increased emphasis on financial literacy and a ramping up by microfinance providers of these "credit plus" services which are clearly needed by rural communities.

ONE ACRE FUND PROVIDES INPUTS, LIKE SEEDS AND FERTILIZER, TO ITS CLIENTS

Microfinance, Inputs, Market Linkages, and Training

Again, Whole Planet Foundation's socially focused partners are already doing this. Particularly in Africa, WPF has a couple of partners who have successfully combined financing with market linkages. For example, organizations like One Acre Fund in East Africa and Babban Gona in Nigeria provide not just financing but also agricultural inputs, training, and crop storage and market linkages. And unlike the trade-financiers, package cost is clearly communicated to members, along with financial literacy.

As the author suggests, promoting financial literacy is key so that customers can differentiate between the various forms of formal and informal finance available and compare the costs and benefits of different services. This is something that WPF's socially focused MFI partners typically deliver alongside their provision of loans and, often, savings products.

Conclusions

Investigating concerns and considering how microfinance programs could be improved are issues of great importance to Whole Planet Foundation. The issue of informal intermediaries seems to flourish in many microfinance programs that are not well governed or managed. Trade-financiers operate in environments where clients have no other options for the farm inputs they need and/or lack the financial literacy to make a different choice.

However, rather than condemn all microfinance programs based on poor management or unsophisticated products of a few MFIs, I believe it would be best to promote the many socially focused MFIs and lending programs that have tightly managed programs, specifically targeting the types of poor borrowers who are otherwise left out. These best practices should be shared and replicated, because, as the authors state, "poverty alleviation requires more than ensuring access to microfinance."

Africa-Middle East and Eastern Europe Region

Chapter 1

Agent Banking in the Democratic Republic of Congo

By Zoe So

VIEW FROM THE FRONT OF A FINCA EXPRESS LOCATION

Microfinance institutions seek to deliver quality financial services to an untapped market: people who are not part of the formal banking system. The barriers of entry to formal banks can be very high, including minimum balances to maintain accounts, transaction fees, and a limited number of branch locations. People who cannot meet the minimum requirements or live far away from the bank branch are effectively excluded from the conventional retail bank services. This exclusion is often by design; retail banks find it too costly and risky to work with clients at the bottom of the pyramid, especially in emerging markets.

Many of our partners, who specifically develop financial products and services for this tier of clients, are turning to innovative technologies to reduce the risks and costs of doing business and improve the quality of services.

Here's one example of a project supported by Whole Planet Foundation, which leverages technology to improve access to financial services.

The Challenge: Absence of, or low-quality infrastructure, such as roads and utilities, means microfinance institutions and potential clients have a hard time connecting.

The Technology: Agent banking with point of service machines.

The Democratic Republic of Congo is the 11th largest country in the world, and the 19th most populous. The Central Bank estimates that only about 4% of the DRC's 67 million people have access to formal financial services. The DRC's density of paved road is well below other low-income countries, due to a history of conflict and a land laced with rivers. How could our microfinance partner, FINCA, reach potential clients who lived far away from a branch?

JUSTIN IS AN AGENT FOR FINCA EXPRESS. HE HAS A POINT OF SERVICE MACHINE WHICH LETS HIM PROVIDE FINCA DRC CLIENTS WITH A WIDE RANGE OF SERVICES, INCLUDING OPENING ACCOUNTS, REPAYMENT AND DISBURSEMENT OF LOANS, AND DEPOSITS AND WITHDRAWALS.

A conventional bank might consider a combination of ATMs and online banking services; but the complicated back-end and maintenance, expense or lack of internet connectivity, high bar for consumer education, and security risks make these options impractical.

A representative of the microfinance institution could also consider managing all transactions directly with clients; but this strategy poses the security risk of traveling long distances while carrying cash. The ability of staff is limited by cost and time constraints.

FINCA DRC's solution was to add an additional delivery channel: agency banking, through biometric point of service machines. Trained third party agents, armed with FINCA's customized, portable point of service machines, help customers open accounts, make cash deposits and withdrawals, make loan repayments or collect disbursements, and learn about different bank services.

To build this agency network, FINCA has invested in customizing the devices and developing the backend system; training and supporting agents; and developing a team of supervisors to oversee this delivery channel. Through branchless banking with agents, FINCA has been able to:

- Increase accessibility to unbanked clients in hard to reach areas.
- Offer clients the convenience of choosing when and where to engage in their transactions, rather than be limited by traveling to a branch during limited working hours.
- Improve security by using fingerprint recognition for client identification; and reduce the need for passwords or identification documents.
- Make information about services and products more easily available outside of the branch.

FINCA first started its agency banking network in Kinshasa, the capital of the DRC, in 2013. Many of FINCA's agents are owners or staff of small businesses operating in permanent locations, such as a provision shop in the market place. The FINCA agency banking is an additional service these agents offer on top of their core business. This approach helps ensure that agents are located in a convenient place for clients. The shop benefits from additional sales due to increased foot traffic.

Using branches in major commercial centers as hubs, they are expanding their networks to communities farther away from branches. As of end of 2016, FINCA DRC's network includes 20 branches and 850 point of service agents; 75% of client transactions take place through a point of service agent.

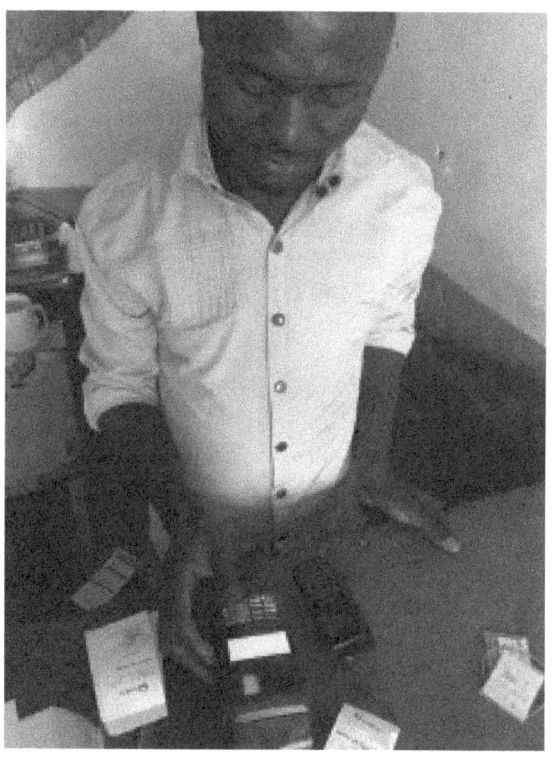

JUSTIN HAS BEEN AN AGENT FOR THREE MONTHS. THE DAY BEFORE OUR VISIT HE HAD 12 CLIENTS. ON AVERAGE, AN AGENT WITH SIMILAR FOOT TRAFFIC MAKES BETWEEN $500-$600 A MONTH FROM COMMISSION.

Although the physical branches are still the anchor for service delivery channel for most microfinance institutions, many of our partners are adding branchless banking channels through use of appropriate technology as a way to increase financial access. The point of service machine is just one of these tools; other tools in the kit include mobile money, the use of tablets and smart phones for data collection; and customer communication through SMS.

Chapter 2

Al Majmoua Provides Outreach to Syrian Refugees

By Brian Doe

RANEEM, A MICROCREDIT CLIENT NEAR BEIRUIT, WITH HER EMBROIDERY FRAMES

At the end of 2017, Whole Planet Foundation had the chance to revisit one of our newest partners in the Middle East, Al Majmoua in Lebanon. WPF is supporting the growth of a group loan program in a country, and region, where loans not requiring an outside co-signer, guarantee or material collateral are rare.

In 2017, Al Majmoua mobilized its staff to make this fledgling loan product more robust and easier to access, as well as promoting it more heavily among the organization's loan officers through increased training and incentives. Today, a group as small as just two borrowers can come together to secure small business loans.

Also, the organization has scaled its outreach to Syrian refugees living in Lebanon since WPF's visit in 2016. The group loan portfolio went from a negligible portion of Syrian clients - about 2% - to almost 29% at the end of the year. There is a huge potential for increasing access to financial services by serving excluded Syrians alongside poor Lebanese entrepreneurs.

One Syrian client we met in the outskirts of Beirut is Raneem who is an embroiderer specializing in sewing intricate designs onto fabrics for women's clothing. For years Raneem has sold her work exclusively to a local tailor that provided her materials up-front in exchange for the sale of all her finished goods.

This year, Raneem has applied for a $500 first loan from Al Majmoua. Payable over nine months, the loan will allow Raneem to buy her own materials and wood framing and increase her market options for her goods. To get the loan, Al Majmoua allowed her to apply with another Syrian entrepreneur and friend who was requesting a similar loan to support her own embroidery work. Al Majmoua has no other requirements beyond showing she is legally allowed to work in Lebanon.

Al Majmoua are seeking to help relieve the economic pressure faced by poor entrepreneurs in Lebanon by targeting niche populations under-served by existing financial services providers as well as providing tailored services for start-ups, youth borrowers, and loans for specialized productive assets and solar energy systems.

Chapter 3

Cash Shortages Create Problems in Zimbabwe

By Zoe So

WPF'S ZOE SO (RIGHT) WITH STAFF AND CLIENTS OF THRIVE ZIMBABWE

A few months ago, I visited WPF partner Thrive Zimbabwe with Daniel Zoltani, Whole Planet Foundation's Global Programs Director. We met many microentrepreneurs who had taken loans from Thrive for their small businesses. Some grew mushrooms to sell in the market and to stores. Others traveled to South Africa and other neighboring countries to buy clothes, or housewares, or other products, to re-sell back in Zimbabwe. Another Thrive client ran a small grocery shop from the front of her house. Their businesses were diverse, but most told us about the same challenge: it was really hard to get cash.

A GROUP OF NEW BORROWERS WHO ARE NEIGHBORS AND ALL FARM MUSHROOMS

When we visited in April, Zimbabwe was in the midst of a cash shortage, and to get your hands-on cash you often had to pay a premium. It cost a lot more than a dollar to get a dollar. There just wasn't enough cash moving around. What does a cash shortage look like on the ground? Some of the microentrepreneurs we met shared their stories.

The Daily Reality of Cash Shortages

Although the official currency is the USD, you are more likely to get ahold of the government issued Zimbabwean bond note for your daily needs. The bond note is pegged to the dollar and officially backed by USD reserves, set at the rate of $1 bond note = 1 USD. But it trades at a much less favorable rate on the street in the parallel market – anywhere from 20 to 30% less. Day by day, transaction to transaction, supplier to supplier, the dollar to bond note rate could change.

For day to day use, especially in rural areas, the certainty and liquidity of hard currencies are preferred and sometimes the only accepted form of payment. Zimbabwe doesn't produce a lot of goods domestically, and cross border trade is popular. Mobile money and the bond notes can't be used outside Zimbabwe's border. Small cross border traders pay highly unfavorable rates to get hard cash in exchangeable currencies like South African Rand and USD.

You might start queuing at the bank early in the morning to withdraw money from your account, money that you entrusted to the bank, then leave hours later with much less cash than you had asked for, or nothing at all. Some banks are said to cap individual daily withdrawals at the equivalent of $20 USD. As a benchmark, a small bottle of water costs roughly $0.68, a dozen eggs about $2, a basic meal at a restaurant about $5, and a bus ticket across country around $7.

Or you could go to a mobile money agent, ask to withdraw the amount in your account, and be charged up to 40% commission. The agents are supposed to honor the official exchange rate: $1 USD = 1 Zimbabwean bond note = 1 dollar in mobile money. But the street rate told a different story, and agents try to make up the difference in creative ways.

All of these steps: trying to get money from the bank or from Ecocash (a popular mobile money system), negotiating the fluctuating price of the bond note, converting bond notes to a recognized currency – come with extra uncertainties and costs.

For WPF partner Thrive Zimbabwe, the cash shortage in the market and at the bank means the best option is to manage the circulation of loans and repayments through the mobile money platform, despite the potential high costs. It was simply the only actionable option.

THRIVE ZIMBABWE STAFF (LEFT) VISITING BORROWERS AT THE WHITECLIFF BRANCH TO CONDUCT A LOAN UTILIZATION CHECK. THE FIELD OFFICER CONFIRMS THAT THE LOAN WAS USED FOR THE INTENDED BUSINESS SHORTLY AFTER THE LOAN IS DISBURSED. THIS CLIENT BUYS CLOTHES FROM SOUTH AFRICA AND RE-SELLS THEM LOCALLY.

How did we get here?

The answer is complex. From the 1990s to 2008, Zimbabwe went through a period of rampant inflation. At peak hyperinflation, prices were almost doubling every day. The government had been responding to cash shortages and other challenges by printing notes with bigger and bigger denominations, like the infamous one hundred trillion dollar note. Hyperinflation rose due to a complex set of economic factors, including the government's decision to print money when the budget deficit could no longer be funded by government borrowing.

The government decided to stabilize the economy by abolishing the Zimbabwean currency and adopting a basket of currencies, of which the US dollars was dominant, as the official currency in 2009. This worked for a while, until in 2016 when there was a shortage of cash in the market. In 2017, the Zimbabwe government printed the Zimbabwe bond note, a decision meant to help with cash shortage issues. The act of printing more money to manage a cash shortage raised red flags of a return to the same cycle of inflation.

The uncertainty of introducing a new form of tender, which doesn't have the protections and foundations of an official currency, caused additional shortages as people started hoarding their US dollars. The challenges and costs of getting cash from banks or through mobile money continues to contribute to more hoarding. Since then political and market uncertainties have continued: Robert Mugabe was ousted from power in November 2017 after 30 years in office, and elections took place at the end of July. The cash shortage continues. But many Zimbabweans see hope in the post-

Mugabe administration's push to make the country a more attractive investment destination.

At Whole Planet Foundation, we are often thinking about how money moves: between people, in local markets, within countries, and between countries. We try to understand these movements to gain insight into the obstacles to financial access micro-entrepreneurs and our partners face. Daniel and I spent one week in Zimbabwe, and every transaction came with a steep and often expensive traveler's learning curve when it came to negotiating prices and payment forms. Even then, we had a lot of leverage with the USD in hard currency we brought into the country. It's still hard for us to fully grasp how small businesses, who have so little leverage, manage to survive in Zimbabwe's volatile market. But they somehow do, negotiating these complexities and still making a little income to help their families, and we were inspired by the resilience of the many business women we met.

Chapter 4

Interest Rate Caps

By Brian Doe

IBITSAM IS A MICROCREDIT CLIENT OF KIEDF, WPF'S MICROFINANCE PARTNER
IN ISRAEL. SHE USED HER SMALL BUSINESS LOAN TO INVEST IN WHOLESALE
CLOTHING FOR RESALE IN HER COMMUNITY.

This week, the Cambodian government finalized a
decision to put a maximum on the interest rate that can
be charged by micro-credit organizations at 18% per
year– called a 'body blow to microfinance' in a 2017 Voice
of America article.

The reaction to this legislation struck a chord with me
after travelling recently to several countries in our Africa
and Middle East portfolio impacted by long-standing
microfinance interest rate limits. I've seen a number of
consequences as a result of limiting interest rates that I

think trusted industry think tank CGAP summarized succinctly: that 'financial service providers find it difficult to recover costs and are likely to grow more slowly, reduce service delivery in rural areas and other more costly markets, become less transparent about the total cost of loan, and even exit the market entirely'.

In February I travelled to Israel where our partner KIEDF is the first best practice microfinance institution in the country and offers small business loans to underserved populations such as Arab Israeli and Bedouin women, with a maximum charge on loans of about 9% per year (neighboring countries' similar social finance institutions typically charge 18% per year by comparison). KIEDF have long lobbied for more flexibility in the charge they can put on their microloans if the country wants to create a far-reaching, sustainable service to the poor.

The program serves clients like Saga, the owner of a small shop, with small working capital loans because she wouldn't otherwise qualify for a loan from a formal bank. Last year, the Jerusalem Post highlighted KIEDF's work bringing services to a population that currently 'doesn't exist in the banking system'. A small uncollateralized business loan of about $1,400 boosts Saga's income potential with a continuous supply of stock for her shop and improved shelving. KIEDF currently supports about 2,000 similar borrowers in the country.

With a limit on the fee KIEDF can charge clients for business financing, the program is only able to cover about 25% of its operating costs with revenue received and struggles to patch together the rest of their operating budget from other sources- often working year-to-year to ensure their program can continue. As CGAP says, this limits their ability to move into new areas, access more costly distant communities and to invest in better systems. KIEDF's low revenue also stifles their ability to attract loan capital from banks and investors to finance their clients- Whole Planet Foundation works to fill this gap with free capital to help support some of their expansion where possible.

I also recently travelled to a very different context, in West Africa, to Senegal where WPF's partner CAURIE organizes women into groups that also receive uncollateralized business loans as small as $100, charged 10% interest per 6-month loan cycle in combination with group savings services. Most of West Africa falls under a regional interest rate maximum of about 24% annual interest while organizations in nearby countries like Ghana typically charge about 36% per year on their social business finance programs.

MANÉ (FAR RIGHT) IS A MICROCREDIT CLIENT OF CAURIE IN SENEGAL. SHE CONTINUES TO BORROW FROM CAURIE BECAUSE LARGER BANKS IN SENEGAL WILL NOT FINANCE SMALL-TO-MEDIUM ENTERPRISES LIKE HERS.

Beneficiaries of CAURIE such as Mané, mentioned in a blog at the beginning of this book and pictured above, are unable to access financing from banks who can't afford to offer such small loans in large numbers and certainly not without any collateral to easily back possible loan defaults.

With the limit on interest that microfinance organizations like CAURIE can charge, it also impacts their ability to operate. CAURIE covers their operating costs with the interest revenue they receive but loan groups often must expand to two or three times the number of members compared to other countries (50-100 women per group versus 25-35 members) due to costs of operations.

Additionally, CAURIE is only able to finance a fraction of the women that have requested business credit from them; typically, they only reach about 75% of the members enrolled in their program at any one time. Lastly, like KIEDF they find it hard to afford and/or attract the actual capital needed to finance their business loan clients, which WPF has helped provide to support some of their national growth.

Not all finance institutions are the same, but both of these programs face operational expenses that require a higher fee on their loans than charged by banks. Unfortunately, the fee that can be charged in these two cases isn't determined by the requirements of their cost to operate but rather by regulations put in place by a local Monetary Authority.

Unlike traditional banks both programs forgo requiring any collateral to receive business financing which requires them to work closely with potential clients through training and orientation and also mobilize a network of field staff to carry out due diligence visits to borrower businesses in often hard to reach places in order to manage the risk of extending credit to the unbanked. It is an expensive way to scale business finance to unreached entrepreneurs.

As CGAP says 'the general idea is that interest rate ceilings limit the tendency of some financial service providers to increase their interest yields especially in markets with a combination of no transparency, limited disclosure requirements and low levels of financial literacy.

In agreement with this, Whole Planet Foundation not only strives to bring business credit to more entrepreneurs, but also to bring affordable loans to places that have been exploited by unchecked creditors. However a 'one size fits all' approach to severely limiting the interest charged on business credit only serves to undercut both objectives. Our partners are unable to both grow their portfolios sustainably, and likely either unregulated informal creditors will find a way to move in and exploit the poor with excessive interest rates or the unbanked will continue to be cut off from accessing working capital to build needed streams of income.

Chapter 5

Bidhaa Sasa in Kenya Sells, Delivers & Finances Beneficial Products to Poor Rural Populations
By Zoe So

We're excited to introduce Bidhaa Sasa, one of Whole Planet Foundation's newest partners in Kenya. Bidhaa Sasa sells, delivers, and finances beneficial products to low income populations in rural areas. Our team likes their client-centric approach to affordable credit, responsive customer service, and attention to internal systems.

Bidhaa Sasa means "Products now!" in Kiswahili. All of their products are selected for their productive time and money savings benefits, and are priced under 10,000 Kenyan shillings, or roughly $100. They currently offer solar products, gas and efficient cookstoves, and maize drying tarps. And they are continuing to test new products to add to the mix. Since they first launched in 2015, Bidhaa Sasa has sold a total of 12,000 products. WPF support will help Bidhaa Sasa reach 4920 new borrowers access these beneficial products.

To learn more about how Bidhaa Sasa works, I spent some time shadowing their field staff in Webuye, western Kenya. I learned they spend a lot of time traveling far distances on foot, matatu (mini-van bus), and boda (motorcycle taxi), to provide a high level of customer service to clients. When staff deliver products to clients, they also take the time to walk through all the features of the product and review the loan terms. Bidhaa Sasa staff also go directly to their clients' homes or businesses within a few days of receiving complaints about faulty products. They'll sit with the client to test the faulty product and try to fix it on the spot with spare parts. If the problem can't be fixed, they might give the client a new product immediately.

WALKING TO MEET CLIENTS WITH BIDHAA SASA STAFF

During our rounds, I had a chance to meet Humphrey, who is a repeat customer and a group leader. Humphrey has taken loans for a Jiko Bora, a gas cooker, and a canvas tarp for drying maize. As a group leader, Humphrey plays a very important role as a liaison between Bidhaa Sasa field staff and other clients. Group Leaders help provide information and demonstrate products to interested borrowers, motivate groups, and recruit new members. Leaders are given small bonuses for their efforts, based on group formation, new clients recruited, and completed loan payments.

HUMPHREY IS A MICROCREDIT CLIENT OF OUR NEW PARTNER BIDHAA SASA IN KENYA.

Humphrey has a store where he sells various daily products. He keeps the gas cookstove he bought from Bidhaa Sasa at his kiosk as a demonstration product in case any of his shop customers might be interested in purchasing their own. He says the stove has helped him save time and money, so he can dedicate more energy to his business. As I chatted with him, a few of his shop customers stopped by. One customer had also bought a gas cooker from Bidhaa Sasa after learning about it from Humphrey. She uses her gas cooker to cook food which she sells at a market in a nearby town.

In recent years, there has been a lively debate about the impact of investing in the energy access sector. Investors are taking a deeper look at the tricky balance between cost, scale, and quality of service to rural clients; and the relationship between such household items and incomes.

To address the first set of questions, many last mile asset distribution companies are relying on technology to manage their loans, such as the PayGo mechanism which enables remote switch-off of products if there is a late payment. Bidhaa Sasa has decided to focus on a high level of human interaction, social networks, and group cohesion methodologies. At WPF, we have partnered with companies who are trying different innovative approaches to delivering credit services to bottom of the pyramid clients.

Whether the model is high technology or high touch, traditional microfinance or asset finance, we've found the fundamental principles of responsible finance remain the same: a commitment to accessibility, affordability, transparency, and customer service.

Chapter 6

Microfinance Emergency Loans
By Brian Doe

REGINA IN FRONT OF HER MAIZE FIELD

Microfinance providers globally are searching for better ways to help their clients, and especially their poorest borrowers, overcome unexpected household shocks that seriously jeopardize the livelihoods of poor entrepreneurs and their families. The sector is only in its infancy in successfully opening up access to financial and insurance products that can buffer the effects of devastating health emergencies, floods, droughts, fires

144

and other events that hurt poor entrepreneurs and their families.

The real impact of unexpected emergencies is often that households are forced to liquidate their personal and productive assets or stop working altogether for a longer than expected period because funds are not available to, for example, access health treatment after an illness or rebuild a home or business after a flood or fire.

Recently, the Asset and Market Access Lab at the University of California Davis and BRAC microfinance with funding from USAID released a short summary of the innovative research they are doing into a variety of products and strategies designed explicitly to help poor entrepreneurs overcome emergencies that threaten to devastate their livelihoods and households. One strategy they present is to offer pre-approved emergency loans that would be triggered when major external shocks such as flooding hit communities where BRAC's clients are located.

I had the opportunity to visit our partner in northwest Cameroon GHAPE which is offering basic group business loans and micro-savings services to men and women in rural Cameroon from their headquarters in Bamenda. The microfinance provider's services are actually quite similar to the microloans offered by BRAC but developed locally in this part of Central Africa. I was quite surprised to find out that built into GHAPE's founding operational strategy was the idea of emergency loans which has been very successful. Each loan group has at its disposal a small no-interest loan fund to offer members funds when needed to cover unexpected personal emergencies that arise over the course of managing GHAPE business loans.

I met Regina, for example, who is a maize farmer as well as owner of a small local canteen and over the course of seven business loans she has accessed through her GHAPE loan Center (she currently has a $170 loan to support stocking her restaurant) has managed to meet the costs of unexpected hospital visits and medicine over the years through very small withdrawals from the emergency loan pool GHAPE offers through her loan group- usually only requiring $10-$20 each time.

REGINA WITH HER GRANDSON HARVESTING FROM HER GARDEN IN PREPARATION FOR HER RESTAURANT MENU

The small emergency loans requests are approved quickly by the other members in her group in partnership with their GHAPE loan officer, cannot exceed about $75 and are expected to be repaid one month later. They also carry no interest. The group has a separate register for tracking and managing this basic emergency loan fund. Beyond being very useful to GHAPE's members it also seems like a service that helps increase customer loyalty and trust in the organization.

This is a solution GHAPE's founder devised in a context where offering health insurance or other more complex loans for non-business purposes wasn't yet practical or feasible. GHAPE is an extremely socially motivated business loan provider and like other similar MFIs is trying to always do better to meet the needs of poor entrepreneurs in under-served communities. It is exciting to see how the sector from the largest players like BRAC which WPF has supported in Asia and Africa to much smaller community organizations like GHAPE in western Cameroon will lead the way in tackling the real challenges faced by their clients.

Chapter 7

Mobile Money Meets Traditional Microfinance in Kenya

By Zoe So

At a microfinance group meeting, you might see a lot of paper: piles of cash, thick record books to record attendance and meeting minutes; repayment schedules; group loan balance reports; passbooks. At the branch office, too, more paper: stacks and binders and file cabinets full of applications and loan contracts.

These documents are the by-products of best practices in microfinance. They are meant to ensure accountability and transparency. But extensive documentation processes can cost time and money for the company and clients, and a high volume of cash transactions can create security and fraud risks.

In recent years, there's been a lot of buzz, and skepticism, about Sweden's efforts to move to a cashless economy. Other countries are following suit. In the place of physical cash, these economies are increasingly using credit, debit, and mobile payments for financial transactions. One central criticism of cashless economies is that the reliance on technology will exclude vulnerable populations – those who are most likely to be unbanked or have low digital literacy or technology access.

What if microfinance institutions could eliminate cash and paper, and still deliver last-mile credit services?

Pioneers in the microfinance sector are harnessing leapfrog technology to do exactly this. Instead of seeing adoption of technology as a barrier for marginalized communities, these innovators are harnessing the power of digitization to expand financial inclusion.

Introducing Musoni Microfinance
Musoni Microfinance, established in Kenya in 2009, strives to provide 100% cashless and paperless services. It serves as the real-world testing ground for the Musoni System. This cloud-based core banking solution is built specifically to help microfinance organizations integrate new mobile and digital technologies to improve efficiency, reduce costs, and expand rural outreach. The interface is compatible with tablets, mobile phones, and computers. It's built to integrate smoothly with mobile

money, and to be user-friendly for clients, field officers, and senior managers.

What does this mean for Musoni's goal? They haven't quite eliminated paper yet. But they are getting closer and closer by focusing on entry level clients.

Whole Planet Foundation recently pledged $500,000 over three years to support the scale of Musoni's most digitized loan product yet: The M-Nawiri group business loan product.

For the M-Nawiri loan, almost everything is recorded and monitored digitally. This includes client profile details; loan applications and approvals; credit history; repayment schedules; repayment reminders. At the group meetings I visited, I often saw just two physical documents: the group members brought a record book, where they keep track of all group meetings and minutes; and the loan officer brought a one page print out of the group's loan balance. There was no physical cash on the table; repayments were all made through mobile money which then directly posts to the loan account.

At one group meeting, the members approved a loan to a new member. The loan officer and other members helped the new client go through the USSD menu on her own simple feature phone to fill out the loan application. This information directly feeds into Musoni's database, which already contained her profile and registration details. This type of digital integration is present in all aspects of the loan process, from registration and application to approval, disbursement, and repayment.

As the microfinance industry becomes increasingly digitized, more and more institutions are adopting tools to help streamline tasks. Many have gone a step further, by using fully digitized, algorithm based mobile money loans in which there's no direct in person contact between the borrower and the bank. The allure of relying more on technology is understandable: wider outreach and scalability without the costs of a physical presence. But often, these loans sacrifice too many know-your-client best practices, resulting in high levels of default and client over-indebtedness.

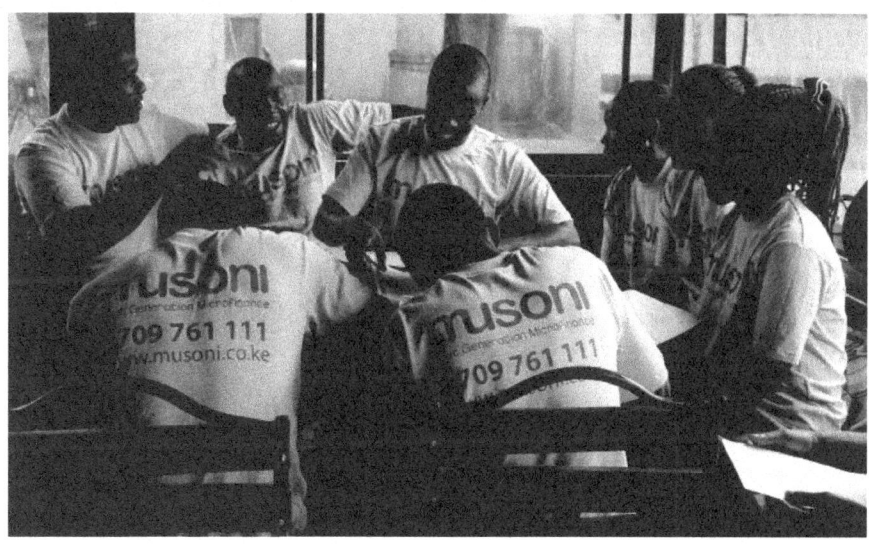

PHOTO COURTESY OF MUSONI MICROFINANCE

This trend is especially apparent in Kenya, the birthplace of mobile money. An estimated 90% of Kenyans own mobile phones and 52% of the total population uses mobile money. Mobile money has been a significant driver of financial inclusion in Kenya. As of 2017, 82% of Kenyan adults held some form of financial account; roughly 25% of Kenyans held only a mobile money account. The growth of mobile money has been accompanied by a growth in financial services. The ease of sending and tracking money has led to a recent boom in services providing quick, near-instant mobile loans. This surge in credit options has also led to what some call a crisis in over-indebtedness, characterized by poor transparency and irresponsible lending behaviors especially affecting poorer borrowers.

In this context, Musoni's M-Nawiri loan uses technology to replace paper and money, but it also steadfastly retains many of the aspects of a more traditional microfinance methodology. Business and home visits, group solidarity, and frequent group meetings are all integral to their loan process. Musoni remains committed to high touch, client centered services despite the competitive pressures in the market.

Chapter 8

New Mobile Phone Services Empower Rural Businesses in Cote D'Ivoire

By Brian Doe

PAMF STAFF AND CLIENTS IN NORTHERN COTE D'IVOIRE

Last month, I went Cote D'Ivoire to visit WPF long-time microfinance partner PAMF, who administers group microloans to rural entrepreneurs and farmers. This visit allowed me to observe the initial roll-out of a new mobile phone-based platform that WPF provided grant funding to help build. The platform will allow anyone with a cell phone to repay loans or deposit savings into PAMF accounts without having to travel to a PAMF branch office. WPF also has provided growth capital to finance rural loans taken by these groups since 2013.

WPF decided to provide a grant for building a mobile platform because while many worry about the burden of interest rates charged on microloans (and much of West Africa tightly controls and limits these rates), for rural customers it is often the cost of getting from a village to a local finance organization that is most prohibitive when trying to afford a farm loan or to make a deposit into a savings account. Mobile phone access in rural communities presents an opportunity to reduce these costs.

TRAVELING BY MOTORBIKE CAN BE EXPENSIVE AND TIME CONSUMING

The High Cost of Access to Finance for the Rural Poor

During this visit, I traveled to villages around the northern town of Korogho to learn how PAMF serves these communities despite the high cost of accessing them and the long distances between the region's villages and the central town centers where PAMF has branch offices. I learned that farmers in these villages pay a minimum of $4 in fuel to go into town each month on their motorbikes to manage their agriculture loans or to deposit savings into their accounts. This cost of travel greatly increases the cost of financing a small rural farm. In addition, it takes upwards of 2 hours to make the round trip into town and the journey on dirt roads wears on their motorbikes.

PAMF's limited operating budget and security considerations for their field staff prevent credit officers from bringing loan disbursements directly out to village clients or from collecting monthly reimbursements of loans where clients' farms are located. It would certainly be too costly for the program to collect very small savings deposits regularly from its over 42,000 depositors across northern Cote D'Ivoire. PAMF field staff typically visit clients three times during the course of a business loan to provide regular oversight of its enterprise loan program and these staff do not handle money during these visits. This is essentially what PAMF can afford to do in terms of visits to village customers.

TRADITIONAL RURAL GRANARIES USED BY FARMERS TO STORE THEIR HARVESTS

Finding Solutions: Group Lending and Mobile Banking

While most other microfinance institutions have stopped serving very small enterprises in rural villages, PAMF first combatted this problem by organizing PAMF borrowers into loan groups that could jointly contribute to cover the cost of only 1-2 members going into town to make monthly loan reimbursements and deposits into savings accounts on behalf of the whole group of 7-15 members. This strategy allowed PAMF to continue serving rural farmers with farm loans that are typically less than $700 per year.

However, another strategy is emerging that can greatly reduce the impact of the distance between rural businesses and PAMF's financial services. In many other countries in Africa, microcredit clients are already making their loan repayments or savings deposits by mobile phone with a system of 'mobile money' managed by cell network operators. However, PAMF found in Cote D'Ivoire that these new technologies with the potential to benefit rural communities were slow to evolve, particularly in the remote northern areas where PAMF is most present.

PAMF decided to make mobile banking a reality in Cote D'Ivoire themselves, so they approached local mobile operators to build out a system where their clients would be able to reduce their visits to PAMF offices. Four years later, after lengthy negotiations, development challenges and multiple program trials, PAMF is training rural farmers on how to access their PAMF accounts with just a simple mobile phone, on a platform they call a 'Mobile Wallet'.

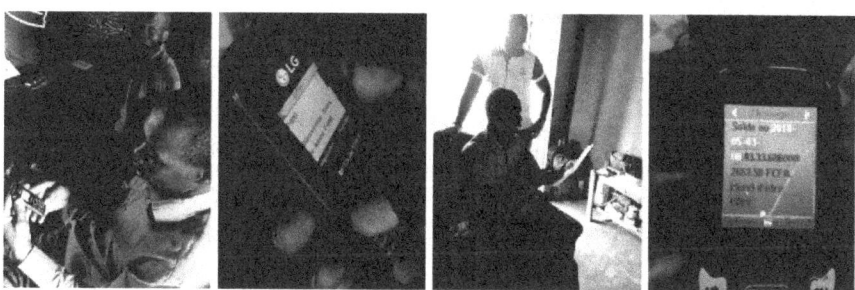

AGRICULTURE CLIENTS ACCESS THEIR LOAN AND SAVINGS ACCOUNTS WITH THEIR MOBILE PHONES

The basic functionality of this new mobile service allows clients to give their cash loan repayments or savings deposits to a mobile money representative in their village so that they can then transfer these funds directly into their PAMF account. Over time PAMF will add more services to the platform to reduce the sums of money traveling long distances across rural roads. PAMF has worked hard to negotiate beneficial rates for making these transfers with a cell phone affordable and the cost of around 30-40 cents per transaction is vastly more affordable than what farmers pay for fuel to travel to a PAMF branch.

In West Africa it is expensive to work in rural communities and there are limited options available to rural businesses seeking capital to grow their enterprises or farms. PAMF is a leader in finding ways to overcome obstacles to access despite the organization's own difficulties to cover high operating costs. Now PAMF will expand access to secure savings accounts and affordable business capital to anyone regardless of their location, thanks to the mobile wallet platform they have launched.

The Future of New Technology in Group Lending

Foremost, the immediate concern WPF addressed when deciding to fund the development of the mobile phone platform was the cost of taking a loan for the thousands of rural entrepreneurs and farmers PAMF is working with. Ultimately, WPF felt the new technology would allow more rural populations to open savings accounts where access is otherwise non-existent.

However, as I learned more about PAMF's mobile banking system, I asked myself: Will new technologies such as using mobile phones to manage microloans change the role of loan groups in microfinance? Will it break down the system of loan groups if each member can send money to PAMF with their own mobile phone?

Recently, I came across this article about a microfinance institution called SAJID in Bangladesh that has also traditionally served customers in loan groups and recently decided to offer cashless repayments with mobile phones. SAJID struggled to determine what the role of their loan groups would be if each member could independently manage their business loans from their own mobile phones.

Ultimately the article (and the microfinance institution) concluded that there are huge benefits to keeping borrower loan groups even when their role facilitating repayments or deposits is no longer needed. The groups still lower the cost of oversight visits by MFI staff, they help with explaining processes and procedures across members, allow for word-of-mouth marketing, and other benefits. At PAMF, the group structure also allows clients to avoid any complex guarantees on their enterprise loans by mutually guaranteeing repayment of the loans.

At Whole Planet Foundation, we seek out microfinance partners that are not afraid to challenge their ways of working to better serve marginalized communities. The evolution of how PAMF in Cote D'Ivoire has continually confronted obstacles to their clients is why WPF has continued to support their work since 2013. PAMF is only starting its roll-out of mobile phone-based services to loan groups in Cote D'Ivoire and it will be interesting to see how their group model will be impacted by these new technologies.

Chapter 9

Reaching Entrepreneurs in Ukraine

By Brian Doe

ZORYANA NOT ONLY PRODUCES CHEESE AND SOUR CREAM ON HER FARM IN UKRAINE, BUT ALSO INVESTED HER MICROLOAN CAPITAL INTO HER ROSE GARDEN

In Ukraine, Whole Planet Foundation is helping local Credit Union Anisia to better serve very small rural enterprises with financing that adapts the successful group loan methodology used internationally, but rarely in Central and Eastern Europe. Anisia launched this new outreach strategy to Ukrainian entrepreneurs by partnering with an innovative new Ukrainian NGO called Key Initiative launched out of a realization that while Ukrainian Credit Unions are trusted local service providers, they aren't reaching their potential to help very small enterprises grow in rural communities.

During a recent visit to Anisia and Key Initiative's new group loan program, in rural towns outside of Lviv, Ukraine it was obvious the impact these small, easily managed business loans were having on rural businesses. Natalya spent years after graduating from school looking for work without success and joined Anisia's new business loan program, receiving about $828 to open a shop that has proven a stepping stone to building a reliable income on her own.

NATALYA JOINED ANISIA'S NEW PROGRAM AND USED HER MICROLOAN TO OPEN A SMALL STORE

Natalya meets with her loan group weekly and repays the capital in small, easy to afford installments. Other group members used similar financing to grow their home farms, start sewing businesses, expand a salon and trade in a variety of products from clothes to furniture.

In Ukraine, trust in the banking sector is particularly low after a recent history of collapsing banks that resulted in widespread loss of personal savings and left few options for small businesses to receive affordable financing to grow their operations. A Credit Union like Anisia, however, is a member-owned financial organization that is controlled by its members and offers savings and basic small loans to participating members as an alternative to commercial banks. Its membership structure lends a true spirit of self-reliance and community ownership that combats distrust in commercial finance companies and banks in volatile economies.

However, many Credit Unions do not provide the strong focus on innovative, accessible loans specifically for enterprise development that WPF seeks to support in poor communities. The technical assistance and support provided by Key Initiative to Anisia has helped bring this focus on microfinance for entrepreneurs to Anisia Credit Union that has otherwise served its members for almost 25 years, offering savings accounts and personal loans.

Zoryana's husband has long been a member of Anisia but it was only through a newly formed loan group that Zoryana applied for and received a first loan of $1,200 to support a range of rural business activities she runs from her own home farm.

ZORYANA NOT ONLY PRODUCES CHEESE AND SOUR CREAM ON HER FARM IN UKRAINE, BUT ALSO INVESTED HER MICROLOAN CAPITAL INTO HER ROSE GARDEN

Zoryana has scaled her production of dairy products like cheese and sour cream which increase the value of milk and she has also improved a rose nursery on her land and sells the flowers in nearby cities. She repaid her first loan and has since invested an additional loan of $1,500 from Anisia's program into the business.

The partnership between Anisia and Key Ukraine has been a success so far and Key Initiative is now reaching out across the country to other Credit Unions interested in launching similar loan groups to help rural entrepreneurs like Natalya and Zoryana. WPF is proud to have Anisia as the Foundation's first partner in Central and Eastern Europe and is now looking closer at other Credit Unions in the region supporting rural entrepreneurs.

Chapter 10

Reducing Risk by Encouraging Resilience in Microfinance

By Zoe So

Microfinance provides opportunities for borrowers to start and reinvest in businesses; generate income; and carve their own pathways out of poverty. But the path isn't always so smooth. Poor households are especially vulnerable to economic shocks, ranging from common situations like illness and death in the family, to exceptional crises like health epidemics, natural disasters, and political instability.

Studies have shown that microfinance's impact is not just a simple matter of enterprise development; it also helps borrowers be more resilient in the face of economic shocks. I had the opportunity to visit two of Whole Planet Foundation's microfinance partners in West Africa whose holistic approaches recognize the importance of resilience to a client's economic well-being. This idea doesn't just make good social sense for the microfinance institution (MFI), it also makes good business sense: a borrower's ability to take or repay a loan will be affected by his or her ability to weather hard times.

Resilience in Burkina Faso

A recent CGAP study in Burkina Faso found that clients of two particular microfinance organizations (MFIs) often dealt with economic shocks using "negative" coping mechanisms, such as reducing household food consumption or selling grain, which had long term negative effects on the household. The report recommends MFIs should be intentional about building resilience, with strategies that help their borrowers mitigate risk.

Yikri, WPF's microfinance partner in Burkina Faso, employs full-time, in-house social workers to help beneficiaries manage personal challenges. Any beneficiary can contact Yikri's social workers by phone or in person, for a confidential consultation about any topic, such as health problems, childcare and school fees, or marital issues. The social workers then help identify locally available resources, like health clinics providing affordable care, and make referrals. Loan officers will often seek the social workers' assistance to follow up with beneficiaries who they think may be going through difficult times. The social workers also help develop training modules based on feedback.

NEW BORROWERS GATHER AT A YIKRI GROUP MEETING, PABRE BRANCH

THE VILLAGE WHERE THE GROUP MEETING WAS TAKING PLACE

167

When I visited Yikri, Flora Diapa, a social worker based in Cissin, told me she has worked on 52 cases in the past five months. Prior to joining Yikri, she had worked on refugee issues and Ebola sensitization and was initially skeptical about the role of a social worker at a financial institution. Now, she works closely with her colleagues to follow up with beneficiaries and develop social-skills-based trainings.

FLORA DIAPA, ONE OF YIKRI'S SOCIAL WORKERS

Institutional Resilience During Crisis

Microfinance is in essence a risky endeavor. MFIs invest in entrepreneurs and environments often considered too risky by larger commercial banks. Institutions, too, need to be resilient so they can adapt to macro-level crises and continue to support economic recovery after the crisis has passed.

In Sierra Leone and Liberia, WPF microfinance partner BRAC stayed with their clients through the Ebola epidemic of 2014, which devastated families and communities, and effectively shut down most economic activity. In an effort to contain the spread of the disease, public movements were restricted. These restrictions heavily affected BRAC borrowers, many of whom were informal and petty traders. Many were left without a viable business. In August 2014, BRAC froze its lending operations for 7 months, during which they did not give loans or take any repayments. In this interim period, BRAC shifted its focus to disseminating health information to communities. BRAC also kept its staff on the payroll with the goal of relaunching microfinance activities as soon as the markets and their clients were ready. BRAC restarted its microfinance operations in March 2015, reassessing and re-scheduling loans on a case-by-case basis.

During my visit to BRAC Sierra Leone, I had the chance to meet with borrowers from the Musu Street Group who had been with BRAC since before the Ebola crisis. This group lives in Kenema, one of the towns at the epicenter of Sierra Leone's Ebola outbreak.

ADIZA, A CLIENT OF BRAC SIERRA LEONE AT HER SHOP IN KENEMA MARKET

I met Adiza, who has a provisions shop and was on her second loan with BRAC at the time the Ebola epidemic hit. She took her third loan in August 2015 and is now on her fourth loan. She said that times are hard now, because of the high cost of goods in the market. Her profit is less than what she was making before the Ebola epidemic, but she still wants to keep re-building and growing her business.

Stories from Yikri's social workers and Adiza's personal account of her experience as a borrower in Sierra Leone help bring names and faces to the concept of resilience in the world of microfinance.

ADIZA'S GROUP (MUSU STREET GROUP)

As Judith Rodin explains in her book, The Resilience Dividend, "Building resilience creates two aspects of benefits: it enables individuals, communities, and organizations to better withstand a disruption more effectively, and it enables them to improve their current systems and situations. But it also enables them to build new relationships, take on new endeavors and initiatives, and reach out for new opportunities, ones that may never have been imagined before."

Chapter 11

Global Fund for Widows in Egypt
By Brian Doe

A MICROCREDIT CLIENT IN EGYPT DISPLAYS HER FRUIT FOR SALE

In 2017, Whole Planet Foundation's Board of Directors approved a grant to support the growth of an innovation business loan program in Egypt supporting widows and other female heads of households in poor communities of Upper Egypt to increase their incomes through self-employment and access to work in higher value home-based activities such as duck rearing and wholesale. WPF will be helping to finance about 500 new women, starting in 2018.

Whole Planet Foundation will be working with the Global Fund for Widows and their local microfinance partner the Future Eve Foundation, to help increase access to business capital for female breadwinners facing extreme challenges in providing sufficient income to support their families. The program which they call the Amal program (Amal meaning Hope in Arabic) focuses their outreach for this loan program to women who are widows, divorced, abandoned by a spouse or in some cases find their husband incapacitated and unable to work.

The Global Fund for Widows has developed this focus on economic empowerment for a particularly vulnerable population in Egypt and other countries. Globally, the 'shock' to a household due to widowhood has been documented in the UK's Loomba Foundation extensive 2010 and 2015 Global Widows Reports showing the particular disenfranchisement, social exclusion and

obstacles to accessing social services that come with widowhood.

Global Fund for Widows works to bring direct support to this segment of the poor and has also found that many of the Reports' conclusions are also relevant to other households headed by women breadwinners in poor communities. They put the percentage of poor households headed by a widow or single mother in Egypt as 36% or higher and is a key indicator of cyclical extreme poverty that can push an entire household into extreme poverty.

Future Eve Foundation is able to support this particularly vulnerable population by hiring local staff and linking with engaging local leaders that can help ensure a close relationship between the microfinance institution and the business clients.

Additionally, Future Eve Foundation have been working with Global Fund for Widows to promote and assist their clients in the program to improve income possibilities through participation in higher yielding value chain activities. Currently clients can choose training and assistance in launching duck-related businesses which are known to be highly profitable in Egypt and easily managed from the home making raising or wholesale of ducks a rewarding enterprise for female breadwinners working to both care for a family and earn a meaningful income.

USA Region

Chapter 1

Why Does Such A Thing Exist? Solidarity Microfinance for Women in the United States

By J.P. Kloninger

MEMBER-BORROWERS AND CENTER MANAGERS AT GRAMEEN AMERICA
BRANCH OFFICE IN CHARLOTTE, NORTH CAROLINA IN 2013

The Merriam-Webster dictionary defines poverty as "the state of one who lacks a usual or socially acceptable amount of money or material possessions."

However, what is "usual" or "socially acceptable" can vary quite a bit from one person, family, or community to the next, and certainly from one country to the next. We are thus compelled to use some sort of criteria or thresholds, formally or informally, to help us define poverty as it exists in different contexts.

While most of us generally consider the United States to be a "rich" country by global standards, and while this is true by several measures, many people in the U.S. still live in poverty. By one widely-recognized, cited, and applied measure, that of the U.S. Census Bureau, 38.1 million lived in poverty in the U.S. in 2018, and while estimates and opinions on the matter vary, there is little doubt that the current coronavirus pandemic is contributing to a marked rise in the number of people in the U.S. – not to mention the whole world – lacking "usual or socially acceptable amounts of money."

The Likeliest and Unlikeliest of Times: Joining Forces During the Great Recession

The United States is one of 77 countries around the world where Whole Planet Foundation is actively supporting the alleviation of poverty through microcredit. For well over a decade, we have been working closely with our United States microfinance partner, Grameen America (www.grameenamerica.org).

Building on the legacy and successful solidarity-group lending model of Nobel Peace Prize Laureate Muhammad Yunus, Grameen America offers collateral-free microloans ranging from $2,000 - $15,000 to women who run small businesses across the United States. Grameen America specifically aims to support entrepreneurial women living below the federal poverty line, with little or no access to credit in the mainstream financial system.

In 2008, when the world was in the thick of the Great Recession, WPF supported Grameen America's first branch office with a grant for $150,000 to increase their microloan portfolio. These operations are in Jackson Heights, a multicultural micro-neighborhood in the borough of Queens, New York. At the time, nearly a quarter of the people living below the poverty line in the US were first-generation immigrants and their family members.

This reality is not materially different today. Of the US's poor immigrant population, approximately half is female. These women are among the lowest paid in the US workforce, yet their economic contributions are essential not only for the survival or upward mobility of their families in the US, but in their home countries as well.

They Emerged, and They Flourished

Today, twelve years after Grameen America opened its doors in Jackson Heights, the organization has an impressive, much-expanded footprint across the United States, with 23 branches across 15 U.S. cities. During that time, Whole Planet Foundation has supported them with $5.7 million in grants for revolving loan capital, helping develop 17 of those branches as they work towards self-sufficiency.

As of March 31, 2020, Grameen America's 23 branches have served more than 132,000 women across the US with over $1.5B in small loans to support their small businesses. Keeping its focus on underbanked women and adhering to the critical elements for success of

Professor Yunus' group lending model, Grameen America has also been able to maintain impressive repayment rates consistently over 99% across their branches' portfolios. This high level of repayments further allows Grameen America to re-lend the recovered loan capital, making nearly all of it available again to entrepreneurial women so they can continue working towards a higher quality of life for themselves and their families, thus adding that much more value to the economy.

Recent Support of Grameen America

The most recent Grameen America branches which WPF has supported with loan capital are in Fresno (the office there opened in October 2019) and Long Beach, California (which opened in September 2019).

Fresno is the largest city in California's agricultural Central Valley; it has a diverse and growing population with significant levels of poverty and low wage working families. Nearly 1 in 4 residents of Fresno County live in poverty (at just under 25%).

The third Grameen America office established in the Los Angeles metropolitan area is in Long Beach, which is the second largest city in that region. The poverty rate there is 18.8%, with Hispanic females making up the largest demographic living in poverty.

Embracing Innovation through Technology

A big part of what has allowed Grameen America to grow its efficiency and impact is their focus on utilizing practical, powerful technologies to ease and accelerate the execution of their model. As one might expect, when Grameen America first began to apply the Grameen methodology in the 21st century U.S. (Professor Yunus developed the model in Bangladesh in the early '80s), they utilized most of the "tried and true" elements of Grameen banking, such as their trademark blue-green recordkeeping passbooks for every borrower, manually-updated accounting ledger books, and cash-only loan disbursements and repayment installments. However, it quickly became clear that adaptation of the model would be needed to have a lasting, positive impact in the new, different culture and environment that is Queens, New York.

GAI HOUSTON BRANCH MANAGER DAVID ACOSTA, PROCESSING A LOAN DISBURSEMENT WITH A MEMBER-BORROWER, APRIL 2019

From that starting point, aided by the application of new technologies, Grameen America has evolved a good deal and operates very differently today than it did when it launched over decade ago. They are now a 100% cashless operation. All members nationwide receive loans through pre-loaded cards which can be used like debit cards, allowing them to expend the total amount of their loan over a series of digital transactions. Grameen America members now repay loans via cashless options and receive text receipts for their transactions. By interacting with digital and cashless systems during Center Meetings on a weekly basis, members build familiarity with and begin to trust digital systems.

By going cashless and paperless, Grameen America's field officers now have more time to deliver education and training to their members.

At WPF, we highly value our microfinance partners' emphasis on, and delivery of, what we often call "credit plus" services to its members. That is, what our partners provide for their clients –including not only loans for their small enterprises, but also education-, health-, and business-enhancing courses, materials, workshops, and more. These "plus" components of an MFI's operations can act in synergy with the loans they disburse (and we have directly seen in many cases that in fact they have), to enable greater and longer-lasting positive outcomes for the member-borrowers, their families, and their communities.

"Necessity is the mother of adoption"

As for most all organizations to varying degrees, the COVID-19 pandemic in 2020 has greatly affected Grameen America's working landscape. It has been particularly acute for Grameen America for many reasons, one of which is the large relative presence they have in New York, with over 20,000 current members in this part of the U.S. which has experienced some of the worst effects of the coronavirus.

As the COVID-19 situation escalated in March of 2020, Grameen America (which is headquartered in New York City) quickly responded to serve the women entrepreneurs they support all over the U.S., in several innovative and practical ways, resulting in the continuation of microloan disbursements, repayments as possible, business advice and other trainings – all for the first time in 100% virtual manner. This required increased utilization of technologies they had already developed and implemented, such as text messages to borrowers to confirm a completed loan installment payment and updated loan balance; as well as activation of new tools and measures to help them continue delivering essential capital and engage borrowers virtually.

In late March, during a call between members of Grameen America and Whole Planet Foundation, Andrea Jung, the President & CEO of Grameen America gave us an impressive, inspiring update, describing how the team has pivoted quickly and effectively during the pandemic. One of Andrea's statements in particular resonated with me: "Necessity is the mother of adoption." As economic activity in cities across the U.S. continues to be greatly diminished, low-income women entrepreneurs and their families have been enduring some of the hardest financial consequences. With the objective of supporting the resilience and recovery of small businesses across this country, Grameen America is doing much more than just continuing their core services with enhanced use of technology. In addition to fully implementing a virtual model of program delivery to support the 52,000 women entrepreneurs they serve, Grameen America has:

- Lowered the interest rate on existing loans to 0%, offering loan extensions to members who are unable to make their weekly repayments, and covering all member costs to digital repayment vendors to support safe, virtual operations. These changes give their members the flexibility to deploy their business capital where and when it is needed the most, with no concern for interest costs or external repayment fees; and

- Launched the Grameen America Economic Relief & Recovery Fund, with the goal of raising $72 million to help them continue providing essential capital and services to their members.

At Whole Planet Foundation, we are impressed and proud of the work Grameen America is doing to support low-income entrepreneurial women in the US. They have re-confirmed for us that a small amount of credit, ideally coupled with the sharing of new, useful knowledge with the borrower, can create disproportionately large and beneficial returns in both the short and long terms -- truly for all of us in our ultra-connected global community.

Chapter 2

Whole Planet Foundation and Major Donors are Alleviating Poverty in Florida

By Joy Stoddard

SOME OF OUR GROUP WITH MICROCREDIT CLIENT YARELI AND HER DAUGHTER, IN HER BAKERY

Whole Planet Foundation alleviates poverty in 17 cities in the United States and 75 additional countries that supply Whole Foods Market stores with products. In Miami, the Foundation supports our primary microfinance partner in the USA, Grameen America. Whole Planet Foundation has disbursed $6,000,000 to

Grameen America to empower entrepreneurial women with financial mobility.

In July 2019, twenty-eight Whole Planet Foundation advocates traveled to Miami to meet microcredit clients and witness the transformative power of microcredit as part of the Foundation's Annual Domestic Impact Visit. Honored participants included **Papyrus-Recycled Paper Greetings** Customer Development Supervisor Andrea Goodman and Account Executive Kelsey Haig, **PepsiCo** Premium Natural Team (**Naked Juice/KeVita**) Senior Director Growth Channels Philip Coughlin and Sales Senior Manager Eric Henriksen, Danone North America, Sales Director – **Natural Channel (So Delicious)** Shawn Bradley with Joseph Jagellio, Lindsey Hamm, Cathy Coupland, Kelly Shea, Bill Sullivan, and Phil Prosia, **Unilever** Director Rebecca Peifer, Team Lead Drew Gostovich, Business Manager (Seventh Generation) John Fitzgerald, **Sambazon** Vice President-Natural Channel Ly Ung, **The Republic of Tea** Minister of Commerce Kristina Richens, **Dr. Praeger's Sensible Foods** Associate Brand Manager Sophia Vitale and Danielle Praeger, **Shoes for Crews** Vice President of Sales Chris Hamilton and Strategic Account Manager Audra Murray, **Grameen America** Vice President of Development Mindee Barham, Development Manager Petra Nelson and Miami Branch Manager Vivian Diaz, **Whole Foods Market** Regional President Juan Nunez and Regional Store Support Associate Coordinator Jodi St. John, **Whole Planet Foundation** Senior Marketing & Outreach Program Manager Sandy Mariscal, Digital Fundraising Specialist Olivia Hayden, Americas Regional Director JP Kloninger and me.

Our two-day experience started with an address by Whole Foods Market Regional President Juan Nunez at the fabulous Whole Foods Market Downtown Miami store, over breakfast. There, Juan shared what Whole Planet Foundation means to him, starting a cascade of veteran and new donors explaining why they work so hard to contribute and be present for entrepreneurs in Miami and elsewhere in the Americas, Africa and Asia where Whole Planet Foundation alleviates poverty.

WHOLE FOODS MARKET REGIONAL PRESIDENT JUAN NUNEZ SHARING HIS EXPERIENCE

Fortified and inspired by collaboration and conscious capitalism, we split ourselves into three different groups to visit microcredit clients Yareli, Marta, Supoya and Kenia.

Our goal was to witness in action different points in time of the unique Grameen America process:

- Group of 5 women forms

- Group undergoes five days of financial training

- Members open a savings account

- Each woman receives a microloan to build a small business

- Groups attend weekly meetings with Grameen America field officers to make repayments and receive training

- Each woman repays loans in full at the end of 6-month terms

- Members are eligible for larger loans to grow their business, build their financial identity, and receive additional support

MICROCREDIT CLIENT YARELI RUNS PAN ARTSENAL HONDUREÑO BAKERY

Yareli's Bakery

Yareli is originally from Honduras, but she moved to the United States 20 years ago. Her first Grameen America microcredit loan was $2,000 and she used that to purchase flour, eggs, and other ingredients for her bakery. She taught herself and her daughter to bake and distributes her product locally.

Her current loan is $3,000 which is used for ingredient purchases. She spoke about how the access to credit helps when sales are down, or for unexpected needs, like a repair.

Marta's Salon

MICROCREDIT CLIENT MARTA OFFERS PROFESSIONAL HAIRCUTS AT HER SALON. PHOTOS COURTESY OF SANDY MARISCAL.

187

Marta has a beauty salon in Little Havana, Miami. She was a beautician in Colombia and when she came to the United States many years ago, she decided to start a beauty business to support herself and her son. She opened her salon 15 years ago. She is now on her second Grameen America loan for $2,000, using it to purchase product and equipment.

Suyapo's Restaurant

OUR GROUP VISITING MICROCREDIT CLIENT SUYAPO'S RESTAURANT GARIFUNYA. PHOTO COURTESY OF KELLY SHEA.

Suyapo's restaurant is located on a corner intersection and serves piping hot plantains with house-made salsa. At night, there is karaoke to draw customers in for a drink at the bar, helping to diversify her customer base. The restaurant was challenged for customers when we visited, so Suyapo was going to work a closing shift that night in order to serve dinner.

Kenia's Restaurant

Kenia opened her neighborhood restaurant four months before we met her, so she is struggling to get the word out, but she has confidence. She said a woman needs to her improve her business not just with delicious food like her Honduran chicken with plantains, but by employing women, to share opportunity.

MICROCREDIT CLIENT KENIA RUNS RESTAURANT LA TAVERNA

She used her first loan to purchase her restaurant food license and said that "a little money helps a lot". She is married with children and says one of her proudest moments was becoming a United States citizen. Needless to say, lunch was delicious!

After meeting these impressive businesswomen and hearing about their challenges and successes, our group then visited Grameen America's Miami branch to see operations in action. It is at the branch location, centrally located for client convenience, that Grameen America collects and disburses loans. Grameen America provides microloans, financial training and support to clients like the ones we met. They get the ability to open free savings accounts with commercial banks and make weekly deposits, and their loan payments are reported to credit agencies, enabling them to build their financial identity.

A MICROCREDIT CLIENT STARTING THE PROCESS TO RECEIVE A LOAN

Finally, for our service component we learned about Hope for Haiti, a non-profit organization working to improve the quality of life for the Haitian people, which impacts south Florida. CEO Skyler Badenoch and Development Director Stephanie Jepsen shared their work with us and guided a Public Health Program activity of assembling 150 personal hygiene kits for women who have no access to medical supplies or medicine. All in all, a great learning experience!

Chapter 3

Whole Planet Foundation and Donors Visit Harlem Entrepreneurs Supported by Grameen America

By Joy Stoddard

CHOBANI JULIET MORAN, IZZE/NAKED JUICE HOPE FURST, MICROCREDIT CLIENTS LANISE AND JANINE WHO CO-RUN THEIR CLOTHING SHOP, TEYSHA ASHLEY LUDKOWSKI, CHOBANI TINA MEHTA, WPF JP KLONINGER, AND GRAMEEN AMERICA RAJITHA SWAMINATHAN (RIGHT).

Whole Planet Foundation has funded microfinance partner Grameen America since 2007, contributing $4.7 million as of March 2020 to alleviate poverty in the United States in 14 cities including New York. Grameen America is dedicated to helping entrepreneurial women who live in poverty build businesses to generate income for themselves and their families.

Our impact visit focus in New York was centered on Harlem as this microlending branch is successfully moving from a research branch to establishing a methodology and center leadership model for African American women born in the United States. In February 2017, WPF authorized a $250,000 grant to Grameen America to support 639 new loans in Harlem over the course of three years. The first tranche of $100,000 was disbursed in March 2017. The average loan size at the time of our visit was $1,500. Loans are made to 100% women clients with a repayment rate of 88% as of this writing. The Grameen America Harlem branch's success in serving the African American community will strongly affect how the Newark branch proceeds, and potential opportunities for expansion into other cities such as Chicago, Philadelphia and Baltimore.

On June 2nd, Whole Planet Foundation hosted our 2018 Annual Domestic Impact Visit in Harlem, with thirty participants including Papyrus-Recycled Greetings (David Sugerik and Renee Sturek), Chobani (Juliet Moran, Rob Igarguen and Tina Mehta), Naked Juice & IZZE (Philip Coughlin and Hope Furst), Seventh Generation (Gayle Grindley and John Fitzgerald), Wallaby (Nicole Duffy), Global CommUnity (Christie Holmes), Teysha (Ashley Ludkowski) and advocates Kristin Meekof and Michael Silvio. Grameen America staff included Mindee Barham, Jill Monum, Rajitha Swaminathan, Tanzila Salahuddin, Latonia Green and Whole Planet Foundation staff included Daniel Zoltani, J.P. Kloninger, Ellen Bettis and me.

WHOLE FOODS MARKET HARLEM STORE TEAM LEADER DAMON YOUNG, WELCOMING OUR GROUP AND EDUCATING US ABOUT HARLEM'S HISTORY AND THE STORE'S COMMUNITY ENGAGEMENT

Our day started at the Whole Foods Market Harlem store with Regional Vice President Paula DiMiglio and Regional President Nicole Wesco who appreciated the group for their commitment to our local and global communities. We were also joined by Regional Associate Store Support Coordinator Mujadila Muhammad, Regional Marketing Associate Carole Lotito, Regional Marketing Associate Lucia Albero, Regional PR Tina Clabbers and Global PR Rachel Alkon.

Because our group was so large, we divided into three smaller groups for visiting local microcredit clients at their places of business. As we meet microcredit clients around the globe, several things are important to create a successful experience for the microcredit client, our first priority, such as:

- Client comfort – the microfinance partners connects with clients who desire visitors and are comfortable sharing their personal story or struggle along with their success and dreams for the future
- Client privacy – always getting permission first to take photos, share business details
- Creating opportunities – the optimal experience is when an authentic interaction like business transactions take place, for example when a client can make a sale to donors who want to make purchases – a win-win! Some of these are detailed below – purchases were made at several of the businesses, including lunch for our group. Another example is when the realities of life help us all relate to each other; every client and advocate wants to have self-value, create income to pay for rent and food, send their kids to school, lift up themselves and their family members.

Of course, we want Whole Planet Foundation advocates to learn first-hand from the client about her experience with the Grameen America approach:

- **Step 1:** A woman with a dream finds four people she trusts to form a group.
- **Step 2:** Groups learn about loans, savings and credit building.
- **Step 3:** She receives a microloan to start or build a small business, allowing her to increase her income.
- **Step 4:** Groups meet weekly to make repayments, continue their education and build support networks.
- **Step 5:** With these tools in hand, women increase their income, build their credit scores, and create jobs in their communities.

- **Step 6:** Women continue in the program and receive larger loans to invest in their small businesses.

MICROCREDIT CLIENTS LANISE AND JANINE RUN A CLOTHING BOUTIQUE TOGETHER

THERE ARE FIVE BUSINESSES CURRENTLY FEATURED IN THE LITTLE SHOP OF HARLEM, AND THREE ARE MICROCREDIT CLIENTS WHO SHARE THE RENT IN ORDER TO HAVE A SPACE TO SELL. MICROCREDIT CLIENT TERRY (CENTER) SELLS LOCAL AND TIBETAN JEWELRY AT THE LITTLE SHOP OF HARLEM. TERRY PROUDLY LET US KNOW SHE IS IN HER 70S AND VERY HAPPY TO RUN THIS JEWELRY BUSINESS WITH THE SUPPORT OF GRAMEEN AMERICA.

A SECOND GROUP WITH CLIENTS AT THE LITTLE SHOP OF HARLEM, LIKE MICROCREDIT CLIENT RENE (CENTER, YELLOW SHIRT) WHO SELLS HER RECYCLED DENIM APPAREL, HATS AND PURSES THERE

MICROCREDIT CLIENT HEATHER IN FRONT OF HER NEIGHBORHOOD HAIR SALON IN HARLEM

MICROCREDIT CLIENT CAROLYN CATERED OUR SOUL FOOD LUNCH OF PASTA, FRIED CHICKEN, STRING BEANS, AND MACARONI AND CHEESE. SHE WANTS TO USE HER NEXT LOAN TO RUN A FOOD TRUCK SO SHE CAN SERVE MORE CUSTOMERS AND MAKE MORE PROFITS.

MICROCREDIT CLIENT REGINA'S BUSINESS IS SHADEESHA'S SWEETS, THE FEATURED DESSERT FOR OUR LUNCH MEETING. REGINA MADE NAVY BEAN COOKIES WITH DOTS OF BLUEBERRY JAM, RASPBERRY JAM AND GINGER, AND SOME WERE DIPPED IN MILK CHOCOLATE AND WHITE CHOCOLATE. REGINA'S PRODUCT TAGLINE IS "THE BEST COOKIES ON EARTH MADE FROM THE EARTH".

After learning more from the Grameen America Harlem team, we then transited to the Grameen America

197

Jackson Heights branch to witness loan disbursements in action. This visit was an inspiring way to see businesswomen making income and taking charge of their economic future.

THE POWERHOUSE GRAMEEN AMERICA TEAM: VP OF DEVELOPMENT MINDEE BARHAM, HARLEM BRANCH STAFF MEMBER, HARLEM BRANCH MANAGER LATONIA GREEN, SENIOR DIRECTOR TANZILA SALAHUDDIN, DIRECTOR OF CORPORATE PARTNERSHIPS JILL MONUM, GRAMEEN AMERICA STAFF MEMBER, RAJITHA SWAMINATHAN AND HARLEM BRANCH STAFF MEMBER. PHOTO COURTESY OF GRAMEEN AMERICA.

All photos courtesy of Whole Planet Foundation and Grameen America.

Part III:

ULTRA-POOR GRADUATION PROGRAMS

Chapter 1

Ultra-Poor Graduation Partnership to Reach 4,000 in Burundi
By Zoe So

Whole Planet Foundation was founded to reach people living in poverty around the globe where Whole Foods

Market sources products. We are excited to announce our partnership with Concern Worldwide in Burundi to support their Terintambwe program, which provides case management services to ultra-poor households so they have opportunities to become more self-sufficient and start small businesses. This project is the foundation's fourth grant in the ultra-poor graduation space. Whole Planet Foundation funding will help Concern Burundi deliver business start-up capital to an estimated 4000 ultra-poor households.

A TRAINING SESSION LED BY CONCERN WORLDWIDE STAFF

Concern Burundi implements a comprehensive two-year graduation program which has several interconnected components. Participants are selected through a transparent and multi-pronged process to ensure fairness and collaboration. Other components include mentoring and training, financial access through the formation of VSLAs (Village Savings and Loan

200

Associations), consumption support, and enterprise creation. Participants develop business plans together with Concern Burundi staff and receive about $84 in start-up capital of for their business idea. Concern Burundi staff members provide business training and coaching to help these new entrepreneurs succeed.

When I visited the rural collines, or hills, of Cibitoke, I had an opportunity to meet with households who were at different stages of Concern Burundi's graduation program. Some had participated during the pilot phase and had already officially exited the program a few years ago. They continued growing their banana trading business and were making improvements to their houses. One participant had started in the program about a year ago and had just received a business start-up capital injection for a small kiosk on a main road. And a few were just a few months into the program, starting to save with a group of peers.

WHEN IN BURUNDI, I MET CLIENTS WHO HAD STARTED A ROADSIDE KIOSK BUSINESS WITH SUPPORT FROM CONCERN'S ULTRA-POOR GRADUATION PROGRAM

Among the participants there were members of often ostracized minorities, internally displaced persons, and orphans who were supporting siblings. Each participant had a different story to tell. But all of them shared similar goals with each other, goals which I believe are common throughout the world: starting and growing a business; helping siblings and children get better educations and better opportunities; and building ever stronger homes and lives for ourselves and our loved ones.

Chapter 2

Funding the Graduation Model in Haiti and Uganda
By Zoe So

PARTICIPANTS OF VILLAGE ENTERPRISE'S PROGRAM IN UGANDA

Whole Planet Foundation is committed to investing in entrepreneurs and entrepreneurial solutions to alleviating poverty, now and for future generations. Since the beginning, we've remained focused on supporting microfinance organizations that target the most marginalized, excluded, or poorest entrepreneurs. But in some cases, households trapped in extreme poverty aren't able to start businesses or borrow start-up capital even from the most socially focused microfinance organizations. Rural areas are often more expensive for microfinance services to operate, and in turn microfinance loans are often too expensive for very poor households living on less than $1.90 a day that have few or no assets.

Introduction to the Graduation Model

To continue to support the financial inclusion of households living in extreme poverty, WPF has recently added two projects focused on the "graduation model." In an effort to identify and review opportunities and barriers around the graduation model, the WPF field team compiled the latest research focused on this growing sector, connected with leaders in the industry, and consolidated our findings as a team. There's strong evidence that the graduation model's targeted and multi-faceted approach helps the extreme poor become economically active and improve their wellbeing.

Just as in microfinance, there are variations of the graduation model practiced in different parts of the world. But most of them share a few common elements. They are structured as sequenced and intensive interventions which often include a careful selection process with community participation, business training and mentorship, and an injection of business start-up capital. The one-time intervention is designed to help a poor household to build assets to engage in income generating activities, as they develop resilience in the face of the unpredictability that often comes with poverty.

Our first two projects supporting the graduation model are with our microfinance partners Fonkoze in Haiti, and Village Enterprise in Uganda. We're excited to introduce these projects to you.

CLM PARTICIPANT AND HER FAMILY AT THEIR HOME. PHOTO COURTESY OF
FONKOZE/MAXENCE BRADLEY.

An Ultra-Poor Program with Fonkoze in Haiti

In 2011, the Fonkoze Foundation piloted Chemen Lavi
Miyò (CLM), an ultra-poor program, to support those
women who were not ready to access credit. Through
CLM, Fonkoze serves Haiti's ultra-poor: those that are
not able to meet basic needs. In general, these women
experience food insecurity, have few (if any) assets, lack
education and have health issues.

Modeled after BRAC's Graduation Model, CLM uses
specially trained case managers to work with the CLM
members over an 18-month period. During this time,
women are taught the skills necessary to create a better
life. At the start of the program each member is provided
with materials to construct a 9×9 meter home with a roof,
floor, latrine and a water filter. Then, each member
chooses two income-generating activities: goat rearing,
pig rearing or pig fattening, poultry and/or other fowl,

small commerce (shop) or agriculture. The members receive the assets needed to start the activities for a total value of $155, a small stipend for 24 weeks and free health care through a partnership with Partners in Health.

After 17 months, each member undergoes an evaluation that determines whether she is ready to graduate. This will be the fourth evaluation throughout the course of the program. She must meet certain criteria focused on her income generating activity, productive assets, savings, health of herself and her family and the status of her home.

By the end of 2017, Fonkoze had supported 6,845 (graduated and currently in the program) ultra-poor families in the CLM program. According to Fonkoze's criteria ninety-six percent of the members that have completed the 18 months have graduated and 30% have then accessed a loan through SFF (Fonkoze's microfinance program). In addition to providing access to credit through SFF, Fonkoze Foundation also supports Village Savings and Loan Association (VSLAs). VSLAs provide the opportunity for members living too far from a Fonkoze branch to open a savings account in their community and eventually the ability to take out a loan within the VSLA.

In 2017, Whole Planet Foundation approved a one-year, $62,000 grant to support CLM. Through the grant, the Fonkoze Foundation will support 400 new members over the course of year. WPF funds will be 100% directed to support the productive asset component of the program ($155/member).

Village Enterprise Supports the Graduation Model in Uganda

Village Enterprise launched their current graduation model in 2011, working with rural communities in Uganda and Kenya. Village Enterprise's one-year program includes microenterprise formation and business savings groups, which help to improve participants' incomes and access to savings.

Village Enterprise focuses on districts and villages with the highest rates of poverty. Participants are then selected through a multi-part targeting process with community participation and using a poverty assessment index. Village Enterprise prioritizes participants who are estimated to live with less than $3.10/day, prioritizing those who live with less than $1.90/day.

Participants of the program form savings groups of up to 30 members and engage in regular financial management and business trainings. Participants then subdivide to form three-person business partnerships. By week 6 or 7, each three-person business selects an enterprise to start and receives an initial business start-up grant of $100. Village Enterprise staff visit and mentor the businesses throughout the rest of the year. After two and a half months, if the participants are managing their business well, the 3-person group will receive an additional $50 capital grant. Businesses are chosen based on market viability and risk level. Some common businesses are goat rearing, bean farming and drying, and maize collection and storage.

In the meantime, participants continue to save regularly through the business savings group. They can request business loans from the savings groups; these loans are managed according to the groups' rules. Throughout this program, participants are practicing group, financial, and business management. They are building assets and generating income.

At the end of the year, Village Enterprise helps groups connect to more formal financial services, such as Village Savings and Loans Associations. Participants come out of the program with increased income and assets, as well as improved well-being in access to food, education, and nutrition.

As of the writing of this post, Village Enterprise has implemented this model in 177 villages in Uganda. They have worked with a total of 87,000 participants, of which an estimated 70% are women. In 2017, Village Enterprise savings groups mobilized on average $44 per member (or $1,324 per business savings group of 30 members).

In 2017, Whole Planet Foundation approved a three-year, $225,000 grant to support Village Enterprise's work in northern Uganda. Through this grant, Village Enterprise will support 1500 new three-person businesses over the course of three years, in an estimated 32 villages in northern Uganda. WPF funds will be 100% directed to support the start-up capital grant component at $50 per member, or $150 per three-person enterprise.

Chapter 3

Preparedness as a Pathway to Resilience in Haiti

By Stephanie Manciagli

EVELYN, A VERY SUCCESSFUL 2016 CLM GRADUATE, POSES WITH THE SHIRT
GIVEN TO PARTICIPANTS UPON GRADUATION (ONE OF HER PRIZED
POSSESSIONS). IN THE BACKGROUND IS SOME OF THE LAND SHE RENTS WITH
HER HUSBAND, TO GROW AND SELL SUGAR CANE.

As new natural and economic disasters arise year after year, resilience and preparedness become increasingly important. With every new threat, families around the world mull over the same considerations: How would we receive warnings in the event of an emergency? How would we obtain our daily medications? Just as we make emergency plans for inevitable shocks, many of us also devise financial projections to ensure our future wellbeing. How will we save for unexpected events? How will we grow our wealth?

In a country like Haiti, with a lack of national social assistance for the poor, households must be self-reliant and proactive to prepare for shocks. Fonkoze Foundation's Chemen Lavi Miyò "CLM" program is part of the solution to this challenge, as they work to support Haitian women to not only to climb out of ultra-poverty but also to prepare for hard times. This 18-month "Ultra-Poor Graduation" program has enabled over 8,000 women (previously living on little to no income) to ensure their families have at least 1 hot meal per day, adequate housing, access to clean water, growing assets, children enrolled in school, proper nutrition and legal identification.

These achievements are the criteria that make up the program's "graduation" threshold and are thus measured before and after joining the program to gauge participants' progress. What is particularly compelling today, amidst 2020's turbulent beginning, is that Fonkoze Foundation recognizes "having a plan" as a final contingency to escaping poverty.

Tools for Progress

Graduation programs provide women living in ultra-poverty with *livelihoods support* (through transfer of an asset such as goats, chicken or small commerce), *social protection measures* (through a cash stipend, health insurance, and social network development), and *financial inclusion* (through participation in a Village Savings and Loan Association, or VSLA).

While each of those 3 elements is vital to the integrated development approach, it is the visits by a case manager to the female participant, to define her most pressing needs, that is critical to catalyze action and preparedness. By co-designing a time-oriented goal with their case worker, the participant commits to progress within 18 months with a clearly defined plan to guide them. This is no easy feat.

When I visited Fonkoze Foundation in January 2020, I met several CLM members who were nearing graduation.

CHIMÈNE SHOWS ONE OF HER ASSETS: A HEALTHY GOAT

One young woman, Chimène, was transferred 2 goats when she entered the program. Soon after, upon Fonkoze Foundation's suggestion, she also joined a Fonkoze Village Savings and Loan Association (VSLA). Working with her case worker, Chimène told him her plan: she'd borrow her dad's horse for several months to make the long trek to buy beans from a mountain-town market.

She'd then sell the beans in the plains, where she knew they'd sell for a higher price. She'd save up her business earnings at her VSLA and then buy her own pack animal, to make market trips more often.

By the time I spoke with her, Chimène was proud that she had indeed saved enough to buy her own donkey, although it took a couple more months than she had anticipated. She even had enough saved to buy a pig. Chimène was concerned when her pig died, soon after buying it, but she wasted no time and sold the meat on credit to her neighbors. While her activities didn't unfold exactly as she had thought, her plan had propelled her forward and equipped her to make quick decisions.

Healthy Networks of Support

Through a collaborative study with the Institute of Development Studies, Fonkoze Foundation found that having support networks contributes to improvement after graduation. For that reason, participants form a life plan that not only outlines how they will sustain an income but that also considers how they will (1) maintain diversified income sources; (2) seek ongoing personal and professional advice; and (3) find emotional support.

Many of the new CLM clients that I spoke with in January were already working to build their networks. Most had between 4 and 8 kids and told me that they had asked their aunts or grandmothers to take in one of their children. Many women were beginning to ask the grown children living with them to contribute to the household. Some were reaching out to the children's fathers, who had abandoned them, insisting that they help pay for the child's care. Such a network to rely on can help women build their resilience and their livelihoods, even in the face of risk.

Fonkoze Foundation ensures that CLM participants' preparation is followed through with by focusing on a variety of hard and soft skills. While it's essential for participants to know how to take calculated risks and have the skillset to diversify their income, it's clear that just having the capital, the awareness and the investment skills isn't always enough. To manage risk, it's essential that the CLM member has the confidence to make a sudden pivot in her business or try a new activity should her primary business become susceptible. Without self-assurance, the woman may hesitate to follow her plan. Testament to their theory, Fonkoze Foundation found that "women who have progressed since graduation are more likely to possess confidence and have a positive outlook...[and] that confidence and a positive life outlook support decisions to take risk, try something new or to rebuild following a shock."

The Poverty Stoplight

During my visit, I was pleased to learn that Fonkoze Foundation will offer participants the Poverty Stoplight in 2020. Having worked for Poverty Stoplight for 2 years, managing their growing international partnerships, I've seen firsthand that the tool can help families reflect on their deprivations and strengths across various dimensions of poverty and helps them take actions to overcome the challenges they identify and prioritize.

Through a self-assessment and coaching methodology, it builds in "reflection" as a response to Brazilian educator and philosopher Paulo Freire's call for "conscientisation."

213

Freire asserts that social transformation requires a progression in which those who've been denied social agency "learn to demand or claim back their capacity to choose." Freire proposes that the poor must be engaged through dialogue and that "the individual gradually will 'become responsible for her own development and act towards addressing the constraining social structures that oppress her.'"

It's clear that Fonkoze Foundation has embodied this approach for years. Now, the Poverty Stoplight should provide Fonkoze Foundation a robust framework for engaging participants in a way that makes each women the protagonist in her story of escaping poverty.

Conclusions

As the world faces new challenges every day, it's worth reflecting on Fonkoze Foundation's poverty elimination strategies as broad lessons we can apply at work and at home:

1. Placing a focus on personal coaching and accessible networks recognizes that the climb out of ultra-poverty (and the climb out of any challenge) requires ongoing support and preparation.
2. Building skills and awareness is critical to growth and resilience, just as self-confidence is.
3. Having a positive outlook is correlated with strong risk management and resilience.
4. Elaborating a plan, one that includes clearly defined milestones and considers the various dimensions of our complex lives, prepares us to endure inevitable challenges.

Amidst this period of uncertainty and change around the world, each person has an opportunity to envision the life they want for themselves, their families, their global communities and their earth. Let's take advantage of this moment to do everything we can to put these plans into motion.

Part IV:

AGRICULTURAL MICROFINANCE

Chapter 1

Babban Gona Partnership Funds Farmers in Rural Nigeria
By Brian Doe

In Nigeria, where Whole Foods Market sources ginger, Whole Planet Foundation offers scale capital to the agriculture social enterprise Babban Gona. Babban Gona is working to make rural farming profitable for smallholder farmers in northern Nigeria. Their founder, Kola Masha, started the business to engage young

Nigerians that have increasingly rejected farming as a sustainable livelihood (read more about this phenomenon in this recent interview with Kola or this TED talk). Today about half of Babban Gona's 18,000 current farmer clients are young farmers growing opportunities for rural livelihoods in poor communities.

ABBAS LEADING A FARMER GROUP THROUGH AN EXERCISE TO VERIFY FIELD SIZE PLANTED WITH LOAN INPUTS

During my most recent visit to the program to discuss the evolution of Babban Gona's outreach across communities, I spent an afternoon learning about new technologies being integrated into Babban Gona's businesses processes demonstrated by Assistant Member Services Supervisor Abbas who was excited to show off the new applications Babban Gona is testing to remotely measure clients' fields after seed had been planted (this certifies that their clients are using their farm inputs appropriately).

NEW TECHNOLOGIES HELP BABBAN GONA STAFF SERVE THEIR CLIENTS

Abbas, however, also explained that he is more than just a Babban Gona staff but is also a farmer himself with a loan from Babban Gona to finance 0.3 hectares of farmland (about ¾ of an acre) growing maize. Abbas took out a microloan of about $100 to finance maize seeds, fertilizers, training and harvest support for his plot of land. When the maize is harvested, this initial loan is extended with a larger post-harvest loan of $160, equivalent to the market price of harvested maize which is put into storage.

This post-harvest loan gives Abbas an additional $60 to finance living expenses until the maize is ultimately sold through lucrative marketing channels established by Babban Gona. Over the next year, he will receive profit payments on additional income earned by his maize above the local market price as it is sold through Babban Gona's market channels. So far in the first half of 2018, he and his loan group earned $75 and Abbas reported that he used his harvest advance loan to purchase additional farmland that will help increase his yield in the future!

ABBAS IN HIS FIELD

This is how Babban Gona turns a traditional farm loan for a very small farm into a highly profitable activity, allowing their borrowers to access better post-harvest prices by aggregating their produce together for future sale to premium buyers.

Babban Gona is a dynamic approach to sourcing quality agricultural produce from traditionally marginalized communities that is changing how a new generation approaches farming and the economic possibilities of their local economy.

Chapter 2

Farming & Finance for a Path Out of Poverty

By J.P. Kloninger

IDE AND FUNDER STAFF AND MICROCREDIT CLIENTS OF FUNDER

At Whole Planet Foundation, we hold that microfinance is not a poverty alleviation "silver bullet," but an important component in a series of factors which can permanently lift people, families, and communities out of poverty. Additionally, because people near the bottom of the economic pyramid often rely on subsistence farming or basic food trade for their livelihood, significant resources have gone into supporting smallholder agriculture in the developing world.

Through a project WPF supports in Honduras, we will get to see firsthand if the two-pronged approach of providing both agricultural and financial assistance will have a synergistic, lasting positive effect on the alleviation of poverty.

With a population of just over 9 million, Honduras is one of the poorest countries in Latin America. About 60% of its people live on less than US$5.50 per day. This is more acute in rural areas, especially among the indigenous communities of the south, the west and along the eastern border. As one might imagine, a great number of these communities produce their own food and engage in farming for small-scale trading in local markets.

During my first Monitoring & Evaluation field visit for Whole Planet Foundation, I visited an organization called FUNDER, which WPF will begin supporting with microloan capital. This partnership provides an exciting opportunity to support small-farmer communities in predominantly agricultural regions of Honduras' Goascorán river basin. The Goascorán watershed is an environmentally and economically critical region in Central America, shared nearly equally by El Salvador and Honduras.

Our Project with FUNDER

FUNDER further partners with iDE, another development entity I visited while in Honduras. For several years FUNDER and iDE have been working closely together via the Nuestra Cuenca Goascorán (In English, "Our Goascorán Watershed") project. With FUNDER's financial products and services and with iDE's technical assistance, thousands of women, youth, indigenous Hondurans and farmers are introduced to new technologies, infrastructure, and activities supporting environmental restoration and the reduction of vulnerability to natural disasters and drought.

FUNDER and iDE improve the livelihood and resilience of food-producing families that are vulnerable to climate change and promote sustainable water governance in the Goascorán basin.

The WPF-funded project objective is to contribute to the reduction of rural poverty in the area. We will provide access to credit to the farmers and members of newly formed village banks in communities throughout the Goascorán region. We will also support them in diversifying their income during the traditional farming off-season. For example, our partnership will provide small loans for agricultural inputs such as seed, fertilizer, and basic irrigation equipment. With the sharing of some technical know-how, the borrowers will be able to produce alternative crops for sale or for their own consumption, engage in new business activities for supplemental income, and create related income streams.

I believe this two-pronged approach can help many, many Hondurans lift themselves out of poverty. I also expect the experience will serve to continue informing us how, sooner than later -- as Professor Muhammad Yunus once said -- we can "put poverty in a museum".

Part V:

BUSINESS IN A BOX MICROFINANCE

Chapter 1

Entrepreneurship in Nepal through the Microfranchise Approach

By Claire Kelly

ONE OF THE KALPAVRIKSHA SURYAMUKHIS (ENTREPRENEURS)

Kalpavriksha is one of the newest social enterprise partners in Whole Planet Foundation's Asia/Pacific portfolio. Kalpavriksha belongs to Pollinate Group and its sister organization, Asha Kiran, operates in India. WPF typically supports organizations who use financing as a means of supporting entrepreneurship for low income communities. Kalpavriksha's program adds entrepreneurship training and links to products that improve health, save time and money for rural Nepali women. It's an innovative, multi-layered program that is sometimes referred to as micro-franchising, MicroConsignment or "business in a box". With a total of $150,000 in grant funding from WPF, Kalpavriksha proposed to scale their network of Suryamukhis (entrepreneurs) from 125 to 400 over three years! However, like other WPF partners, Kalpavriksha is currently adapting operations in response to the COVID -19 pandemic.

The Mission of Pollinate Group

Pollinate Group empowers women as leaders of change to distribute products that improve health, save time and save money for the world's most neglected communities. Teams in India and Nepal identify, train and develop entrepreneurs in urban and rural communities to serve their peers. Entrepreneurs earn respect and meaningful income and become role models who raise awareness about better alternatives. Unlike other last-mile distributors, Pollinate Group's entrepreneurs can earn up to seven times the informal wage.

Asset Finance & the Microfranchise Approach

The majority of WPF's partners implement a Grameen style microcredit program. Sometimes WPF's partners distribute assets (such as solar lamps or agriculture inputs) on finance, rather than cash loans. Microfranchising or "Business in a box" is a further variation on asset finance. The general idea is that the WPF partner provides a business starter kit on credit, rather than a cash loan or asset. At Kalpavriksha, the "business in a box" is a combination of entrepreneurship training and a credit line to access quality household products to sell in their communities. The credit line starts at about $27 and includes a range of small ticket items (such as sanitary pads and LED lightbulbs). The margin from each sale is split between the entrepreneur and Kalpavriksha. In this way, the entrepreneur earns income and Kalpavriksha offsets their operating costs. (Another variation on microfranchise can be found through a rental scheme offered by WPF partner Jiro-Ve in Madagascar.)

SABITRI, ONE OF THE KALPAVRIKSHA SURYAMUKHIS (ENTREPRENEURS)

Promoting Entrepreneurship

Nepal is among the least developed countries in the world. Access to reliable electricity and safe cooking practices are particularly challenging in rural areas. Traditional communities also have deep-rooted social attitudes which leads to gender inequality that worsens the impact of poverty on women. However, Kalpavriksha seeks out low income women to join their program as entrepreneurs. Therefore, the first step is a series of trainings to prepare the participants for a sales job. These jobs are not always easy; to make sales some of the Suryamukhis cover a lot of ground, often on foot or by bicycle, carrying backpacks filled with products. The training process serves dual purposes of self-selecting engaged participants and providing practical training.

Kalpavriksha also has an innovative mentorship program where the Suryamukhis can learn from each other. As the entrepreneurs complete trainings and successfully access increasing credit lines, they work with Kalpavriksha to set up their own stationary business, and have the option to join the team as a full-time staff, training and supporting new entrepreneurs.

Promoting Access to High Quality Products

Besides increased income for the Suryamukhis, the end customers benefit by accessing high quality products. These products typically provide value in terms of health, money saving and/or time saving to the customer. For example, a solar lamp allows a household to work, cook and study after sunset. Kalpavriksha sources products in bulk and they strive to either meet or beat the market price. And, because the Suryamukhis travel to their customers, the customers don't have the time/expense of traveling to the market.

Promoting Women's Leadership

The co-founder of Kalpavriksha Greater Goods, Sita Adhikari, has spent many years working in community development. Her goal was not only to support additional income for the Suryamukhis, but the company strives to promote women's empowerment. One of the key measures for doing this is encouraging the entrepreneurs to take on community leadership roles. According to the survey in the 2016-2018 Impact report, 79% of the Suryamukhis surveyed said they had taken on additional leadership roles in their communities after joining Kalpavriksha. Nearly all women said they have gained more respect because of operating their own businesses.

Managing COVID-19

Like other WPF partners, Kalpavriksha has recently faced some challenges with their primary business model due to local movement restrictions. The local teams are checking in with entrepreneurs regularly via WhatsApp or by phone, prioritizing the health and safety of the women, while confirming their location and the status of collections. Pollinate Group has also been listening to the entrepreneurs' needs and, before the lockdown in Nepal prohibited community visits, provided products such as soaps, handwash and masks. Unfortunately, they have encountered inflated prices when sourcing some critical items. As a result, Pollinate Group is not taking a margin at all in these transactions.

Besides looking after the team and adjusting their immediate product offering, Pollinate Group and Kalpavriksha are leveraging the trust and relationships built in these communities over time to be a two-way source of information during the crisis. For example, sharing reliable information about the virus and symptoms, as well as health and WASH information.

The skills the Suryamukhis have gained are translating to helping their communities in crisis. When Suryamukhi Radha found out two young men who had returned from abroad were unwell in her community, she reached out to them and explained why it was necessary for them to see a doctor. The young men tested negative, however it is a great example of Suryamukhis spreading awareness, even though they cannot visit homes to sell products.

"Our goal is to continue to serve the hardest to reach communities, to continue addressing the inequality gap that is intensified by COVID-19, and create impact in a way that is safe and makes sense in this climate. We are ensuring our entrepreneurs are continually supported during this time, while also ensuring our business continuity - that is, we are here for the long haul and look forward to delivering services with our entrepreneurs in the communities, as soon as this is behind us," says Pollinate Group CEO Sujatha Raman.

Chapter 3

WPF Partner Jiro-Ve, Innovating Affordable Lighting Solutions in Madagascar
By Zoe So

Many social enterprises focus on innovation of high-quality products designed to reach low-income customers. By the numbers, this bottom of the pyramid strategy to reach impact and market at scale seems to make sense – analysis of World Bank data from 2011 shows that 71% of the world's population can be considered poor or low-income. But it's one thing to design a product which ticks all the boxes: affordable, durable, user-friendly, technologically appropriate, and

229

socially beneficial. It's a whole other challenge to get those products to market and to manage a high volume of small sales. Social enterprises often encounter a last-mile distribution challenge: how to effectively deliver, market, service, and finance new technologies to a risk-averse, low-income client base in an environment with poor infrastructure.

The microfinance approach tackles this last mile distribution challenge by delivering socially responsible financial services to customers who can't access retail financial services. Mobile money is another related innovation which taps into this idea. We've written previously about some of our partners in Africa who are bringing high quality agricultural inputs to smallholder farmers. On their own, these farmers do not have the leverage or access to markets needed to negotiate the best prices when purchasing inputs or selling products.

In Madagascar, WPF's microfinance partner Jiro-Ve has developed a creative approach to meet the last mile distribution challenge for getting safe, affordable lighting solutions to low-income households. Here's how it works:

During the day, Jiro-Ve franchisees, who are independent entrepreneurs, charge their solar lamps using solar panels or the main electric grid. On average, each franchisee manages a stock of about 153 lamps. Some franchisees have as many as 500 lamps.

Using franchisees helps Jiro-Ve develop a flexible community-based delivery channel that can be scaled.

Franchisees and their assistants take the fully charged lamps to distribute to clients in the hours before sundown. Distribution usually takes place between 4pm-6pm.

This door-to-door service gives Jiro-Ve entrepreneurs a chance to directly check in with their customers on a daily basis and indirectly market to other potential customers.

At night, the solar LED lamps bring light to households and businesses. Without solar lighting, these customers would rely on candles or kerosene, which provide less light, give off toxic fumes that affect people's health and can cause fires, especially in households with small children.

The rental fee for the basic solar lamp, pictured above, is 200 Malagasy ariary per lamp ($0.06), per night -- comparable to the amount a household would spend on candles or kerosene. This lamp has three different brightness levels and can provide light all night on just one charge.

The next morning, from around 6:30am onwards, Jiro-Ve franchisees and their assistants walk through the marketplace and to customers' homes to collect payment and the lamps. The franchisee keeps 35% of the generated revenue. The remaining 65% goes to Jiro-Ve and helps cover the cost of the lamps, repairs, marketing assistance, training, and overheads.

This approach tackles the issue of financing on two levels: The franchisee gets the assets and services on credit from Jiro-Ve, repaying the cost of the lamp over time. The clients are able to rent the lamps on a nightly basis, without having to take on the risks or costs of ownership.

After seeing the success of their solar-lamp rental program, Jiro-Ve is now piloting a few products targeted at different segments of the market: an upmarket solar home system, and a cheaper rechargeable battery service.

Part VI:

FOOD FROM THE FIELD

Chapter 1

Sopa Paraguaya
By J.P. Kloninger

ILDA IS A MICROCREDIT CLIENT OF FUNDACIÓN PARAGUAYA

You'll need a fork to eat this soup, and you'll love it!

It must have been a chilly evening circa 1845 in Asunción, Paraguay, when President Carlos Antonio López was heading home for dinner, very much looking forward to his daily bowl of tykueï, a white soup made with milk, cheese, corn flour, and eggs.

The *machú* (cook) was not having the best of days. In her rush to have dinner ready for don Carlos, she added too much corn flour to the tykueï and the preparation was much too thick. In her frenzy to finish all the dishes in time, in a moment of fear mixed with ingenuity, the machú decided to pour the mixture in an iron pot and place it in the tatakuá (a semispherical wood-fired clay oven).

About an hour later, President López sat at his table, happy to see the spread of food in front of him. However, his favorite soup was missing and instead, he noticed something served that appeared to be some kind of cake or loaf of bread. When asked about this, the machú explained what had happened to the tykueï. Skeptically, don Carlos tried the bread, and found it delicious! Right then and there, he proclaimed this new dish would henceforth be called Sopa Paraguaya (Paraguayan soup).

Whether this story is true or not, there is no doubt that Sopa Paraguaya is a traditional Paraguayan form of cornbread, still enjoyed all over the country's homes and restaurants.

One of my "happy places" occurs where and when good food and microfinance intersect. This most certainly happened last August, thanks to Ilda Colli and her delicious Sopa Paraguaya.

Early August 2018, in the district of Mariano Roque Alonso, part of the Gran Asunción, Paraguay metropolitan area, I had the pleasure of meeting doña Ilda at her roadside restaurant, "Comedor 42" ("Eatery 42"). She told me she decided to keep the name it had at its original location, which was next to Bus Station number 42 just a few miles away.

Twenty-three years ago, Ilda was a struggling cook at the original Comedor 42, which was then owned by an older gentleman. One day back then, somewhat mysteriously, the owner visited Ilda's home and asked her if she would take over the restaurant, since he had to leave town indefinitely, the very next day. Startled and excited, Ilda accepted the offer and by that twist of fate became the new owner of Comedor 42. She has not seen or heard of the original owner ever since.

Since that twist of fate, to gradually grow and improve her business, Ilda has obtained twelve microloans from Fundación Paraguaya, Whole Planet Foundation's partner in Paraguay. She obtained her first microloan for 500,000 Guaraní (about 84 dollars) and due to responsible use and repayment of her loans over that last sixteen years, Ilda has built an excellent credit record, enabling her to more recently obtain a loan of 6 Million Guaraní (about US$1,000). Today the restaurant is a thriving local roadside eatery, much favored by locals and highway passers-by. They offer traditional Paraguayan home cooking, which of course includes Sopa Paraguaya.

Recipe for Sopa Paraguaya
(Paraguayan Cheese Cornbread)

Ready in approximately 70 minutes

Serves 6-8

Ingredients:

- 8 tablespoons butter
- 1 large sweet onion, finely chopped
- 1 cup cottage cheese
- 1 cup grated muenster cheese or 1 cup other mild cheese
- 2 cups cornmeal
- 2 cups corn kernels, grated or 1 (16 ounce) can cream-style corn
- 1 teaspoon salt
- 1 cup milk
- 6 eggs, separated
- Optional: 1 banana leaf to place in the bottom of the baking pan

Instructions:

1. Heat half the butter in a skillet and cook the onions over moderate heat until tender but not brown. Set aside.
2. Combine the remaining butter with the cottage cheese and mix until thoroughly combined.
3. Add the Muenster, onions, cornmeal, corn, salt, milk, egg yolks, and mix thoroughly.

4. Beat the egg whites until soft peaks form and fold them into the batter.
5. Pour the batter into a greased and floured 10 inch by 13 inch (25 cm x 30 cm) baking pan (optionally, you can line the bottom of the pan with a fresh, rinsed banana leaf before pouring the batter into the pan).
6. Bake in a preheated 400°F (200°C) oven for 45 to 55 minutes, or until a toothpick inserted in the center comes out clean.

In Paraguay, this is traditionally served as an accompaniment to soups and grilled meats, but it also makes a great addition at the breakfast or brunch table. ¡Buen provecho!

Chapter 2

Adventurous Eating in Mexico: Escamoles

by Roxana Newton

PRO MUJER'S HEADQUARTERS IN MEXICO ARE IN PACHUCA, A CITY ABOUT AN HOUR AND HALF FROM MEXICO CITY

Growing up in San Antonio, Texas, I have been in love with Mexico and its food and culture since I was a kid, so needless to say, I was thrilled to have the opportunity to visit Mexico and our microfinance partner, Pro Mujer in Mexico, in September.

I consider myself a fairly adventurous eater and have a pretty tough stomach, so I don't say no to too much. When visiting with Pro Mujer's management team in the city of Pachuca, we decided to head down the street to a beautiful restaurant, El Parador de San Javier. While I was tempted to order the paella, I followed the team's lead and ordered the traditional (and seasonal) dish: chiles en nogada – a sweet and savory dish garnished with pomegranate seeds.

While delicious, what really blew me away was the dish pictured here — *escamoles*! ...or in English, ant eggs!

The dish was ordered as a surprise appetizer for the rest of the table (the person who ordered it was the only one at the table who had eaten them or even knew what they were). After he told the rest of us that they were in fact ant eggs, I Googled it because quite frankly the eggs appeared bigger than actual ants!

Sure enough, they were actually ant eggs, and they were delicious. I didn't ask for the recipe, but the dish was served cold with serrano peppers, onions and garlic (and the all-important homemade corn tortillas). You can find several different recipes on Google, but I am afraid it will be rather difficult to find the eggs here in the United States. Therefore, I encourage everyone to take a trip to Mexico and try some escamoles!

Chapter 3

Fall Flavor: Guatemalan Pepián Stew

by Roxana Newton

Perfect for cool fall weather, this recipe is inspired by Whole Planet Foundation microcredit client Anita from Guatemala.

For more unique recipes from microcredit clients, pick up a copy of <u>Liberation Soup & Other Recipes from Microentrepreneurs around the Globe</u> on Amazon.com!

Anita's Story

Anita is 58 years old and had been a borrower of Whole Planet Foundation microfinance partner Banrural

Grameen for about one year when our field team visited her restaurant. She started with a loan of 1,500 Quetzales (about $194 USD) to invest in her small restaurant located in Sololá, just up the hill from the picturesque town of Panajachel overlooking Lake Atitlan. She has been in the restaurant business for 20 years in various different places.

ANITA SHOWS OFF HER SPICY CHICKEN STEW

Anita has a small but popular restaurant on a main street where she mostly sells popular Guatemalan lunch dishes like Pepián as well as fried chicken, grilled meats, and soups.

Recipe for Pepián Stew

Ingredients:

- 3-pound chicken cut into pieces
- 3 cups chicken broth
- 1 teaspoon salt
- 2 large tomatoes, chopped or 1-14 ounce can
- 5 medium tomatillos, chopped
- 1 pasilla chile, chopped
- 1 guajillo chile, chopped
- ½ cup chicken broth
- ½ cup sesame seeds
- 1 tablespoon of pepitas (shelled pumpkin seeds)
- 1 teaspoon cinnamon
- 1 teaspoons red pepper flakes
- 2 cups chicken broth
- 3 corn tortillas cut into pieces
- ¼ teaspoon achiote paste

Instructions:

1. Place chicken, broth and salt in a large pot and bring to a boil. Reduce heat and simmer for 30 minutes.
2. Bring tomatoes, tomatillos, and both chiles to a boil in ½ cup of chicken broth; reduce heat to simmer for 10 minutes. Remove from heat and let cool while doing the next 2 steps.
3. Toast sesame seeds, pepitas, cinnamon, and red pepper flakes in a dry skillet over low heat. Once you start to smell them toasting remove from the heat.

4. Place toasted ingredients in a blender and pulse to a powder, then add to the tomato mixture and pour back into the blender and puree.
5. Soften achiote paste in a ¼ cup of the hot chicken broth and blend with a fork.
6. Add tortillas, achiote paste, and 2 cups of chicken broth to the blender and process until smooth.
7. Pour the contents of the blender into the chicken pan, stir and simmer over low heat for 15 minutes until sauce has thickened.
8. Serve with warmed corn tortillas and rice
9. Enjoy!

Chapter 4
Suya: A Nigerian Dish
by Zoe So

For me, it's a slice of Carvel ice cream cake or a sip of Yakult. For my mother-in-law, homemade pickled vegetables, only available according to season. For my husband, Toblerone, a gift from a visitor hailing from faraway lands. These foods, once awe-inspiring childhood treats, may now be commonplace in our lives because of adulthood, commercialization, and globalization. Our palates may have changed since then too, and we may now prefer other foods. And yet a little taste still evokes a little bit of excitement and joy.

I started thinking about nostalgic childhood treats because of a conversation about suya. Suya is a Nigerian dish which consists of thinly sliced meat which is coated with spices, threaded on skewers, and grilled. Sometimes the spice mix includes ground peanuts, for that extra flavor and crunch. It is a common street food. Spicy, crunchy, juicy, and immensely snackable. It's popularly prepared using beef, but can also be made with other meats, like chicken, and with organ meat too. Delicious.

The first time I visited Nigeria, which was last year, I didn't try any. I didn't even know suya existed. The second time I visited, just a few month ago, I decided to embark on a side quest to taste the very best suya. I discovered that suya is considered to be originally (or perhaps most masterfully) prepared by the Hausa people in northern Nigeria. Luckily for me, I spent a few days in the Hausa lands in Zaria. Not too far from the still functioning Palace of the Emir of Zazzau, a Hausa emirate with a long and storied history, my hosts and I sat down in the garden of the Suya Spot. By the road, on a raised table, was a huge pit with a fire. Pitmasters walked around the fire, arranging skewers of meat – whole chickens, thinly sliced beef – and grilling them to perfection. Our assorted beef, chicken, and liver orders arrived off the skewer, wrapped in newspaper, with extra spices and raw onions.

I had suya a few more times during my one week stay in Nigeria. On the last occasion, a friend took me to a suya spot in Surulere, Lagos. Side of the road; a handwritten sign listing three or four menu items; a couple chairs and tables in the front all filled; a wandering guitarist and an artist/singer busking table to table. My friend told me he was very happy that I loved the suya. So I asked him, why do you love it so much? He said, "Suya don't really have a way to be described. We grew up thinking it was special meat." For special occasions? "It's an everyday special."

I loved this idea of the everyday special, the way we, our families, and our memories, can imbue a sense of the extraordinary in the ordinary. By doing so we remember to appreciate the context and history and hard work that goes into seemingly everyday objects. And so I started thinking about childhood treats, about ice cream cakes and pickles and duty-free chocolates.

Chapter 5

Chai: The Way it is Supposed to Be

My name is Felicia. I am the bakery buyer at the Davie, Florida Whole Foods Market store. I am an avid lover of chai tea, constantly looking for the best blend, even making my own concentrate.

In September 2015, I went to India with the Whole Foods Market Team Member Volunteer Program, where I met with amazing suppliers, encountered strong women benefitting from microloans funded by Whole Planet Foundation and played the day away with industrious orphans supported by the Miracle Foundation.

One of my favorite experiences was drinking the chai, which could be found everywhere, and each stall or vendor was slightly different. Every time I could have some, I did. What I really loved was sharing the things that connect us as humans.

You walk up to a tiny shop on the side of the street. There is an open coal fire and a large cauldron of boiling water with various spices and tea leaves simmering away. You pony up your 10 Rupees (the equivalent of maybe 15 cents) and watch as the man in the stall lifts the mixture out of the pot in a large square of cheesecloth. He squeezes the goodness out and adds to boiling milk, serving it to you screaming hot.

You love chai, and immediately burn your tongue until you learn the secret. Not only does pouring a little amount into the saucer cool it immediately, it also enhances the flavor as you slurp. Since the tiny cups are not disposable, you sip on the side of the street. Enjoying the day. Enjoying the company. Getting some looks, although none unkind.

This is chai the way it should be.

PART VII

HEALTH, SANITATION, COVID-19 & MICROFINANCE

Chapter 1

Sanitation Microfinance in Asia
by Claire Kelly

ALONG WITH HER BUSINESS LOAN, LUNNIELA WAS ALSO ABLE TO TAKE A SANITATION LOAN FROM NWTF TO FINANCE THE CONSTRUCTION OF A LATRINE IN HER HOME

Whole Planet Foundation's microfinance partner in Indonesia, KOMIDA, analyzed their client information and determined that about 60% of their clients did not have access to sanitation in their homes. Therefore, in an effort to better adapt their services to their clients' needs, KOMIDA piloted a sanitation loan product in 2014 and officially began implementing the product in 2015.

The sanitation loan provides clients with the lump sum cash they need to build a latrine, allowing them to repay the MFI in small installments over time, making the latrine affordable. KOMIDA also provides technical expertise for quality construction. KOMIDA's product was developed with water.org and is being rolled out throughout KOMIDA's branch network as local technicians are trained and on-boarded. As of September 2016, the organization had disbursed in total almost $2 million in sanitation loans to a total of 6,781 KOMIDA clients. They plan to continue to scale up the program.

Sanitation loans are already offered in some of the first WPF-funded branches and the product will reach some of the newer WPF-funded branches in Kalimantan next year. If you visit the KOMIDA website, you can see the details of the sanitation loan product.

Another Whole Planet Foundation partner who has partnered with water.org to develop a sanitation product is Negros Women for Tomorrow Foundation (NWTF), WPF's partner in the Philippines. For example, NWTF client Lunniela, who is pictured at the top of this post with her husband, first borrowed from NWTF to help expand her business. She invested about $106 in her shell craft business to supplement her family's income. Along with her business loan, Lunniela was also able to take a sanitation loan from NWTF to finance the construction of a latrine in her home, pictured below. The sanitation loan is often called a WASH loan which stands for "water, sanitation and hygiene."

At NWTF, local masons recommended by the clients are trained in toilet or latrine construction. Often a client's husband will go through the training and do the construction himself. While the loan is disbursed in cash to the client, the mason also signs the contract to clearly indicate who will be the one responsible for buying the materials (it could be either). Different packages range from 6000-10,000 PHP (≈$133-$233), and the average loan size is $200. At NWTF, clients pay the same interest they would normally pay on a business loan and also a fee of about $6-8, which covers the training and certification of technicians. Loans can be repaid over periods of 3 months up to 2 years.

NWTF started disbursements in July/August of 2015 and as of the writing of this post, they are disbursing about 3-400 WASH loans/week across their operations. In the WPF-funded project area of Eastern Samar, Whole

Planet Foundation capital is used to finance all of the branches' loan products, including the WASH/sanitation product.

According to a recent WSP and Water.org report, lending for household water and sanitation products can leverage dollars invested by 10x. This is because of increased health outcomes and gains in time and productivity. When MFIs provide financing for sanitation products, it makes them affordable to people who couldn't pay upfront. According the report, water.org's global portfolio finds that about 80% of sanitation loans are made to households at the $2/day level.

Chapter 2

Water and Sanitation Microfinance from KOMIDA in Indonesia

by Claire Kelly

WAHYU IS A MICROCREDIT CLIENT OF KOMIDA IN INDONESIA. HER BUSINESS IS TAILORING.

According to The World Bank, approximately 20% of the world's population does not have a toilet in their home. Cost can be one challenge. According to CGAP, "In Indonesia, for example, connection to piped water systems averages $150, while a flush toilet can cost around $250. For comparison, 11 percent of Indonesians live on less than $27 per month."

As Waldron and Shabbir point out in a recent study, while microfinance organizations (MFIs) typically provide financing of this size to low income people, the financial service providers lack expertise in sanitation or construction. MFIs usually provide business loans so that a borrower will have the opportunity to invest in a business with profits to repay the loan. While a water connection will provide a family with long term savings in term of health and time, it will not provide cashflows.

Back in 2014 when WPF's partner in Indonesia, KOMIDA, found that 40% of their own clients lacked a toilet, they wanted to address sanitation specifically as part of their social mission. KOMIDA partnered with water.org for technical assistance to create a loan product adapted for their members and to train staff about how to promote and monitor its implementation.

Water.org has 25 years of experience in the sanitation sector, working in 12 different countries. Water.org partners, including KOMIDA, have disbursed over 2.9 million total loans for 10,256 borrowers as of September 2018, with a repayment rate above 99%!

The partnership with KOMIDA has created a new Sanitation loan product which is specially designed to make it more affordable for members.

- Clients can only take a water sanitation loan after 1 year of membership. This means that the water sanitation loan will be paired with the client's established business.
- Interest rates are cheaper than the business loan and processing fee is waived.

- The loan term can be extended up to 2 years, keeping the weekly installment size small and manageable.

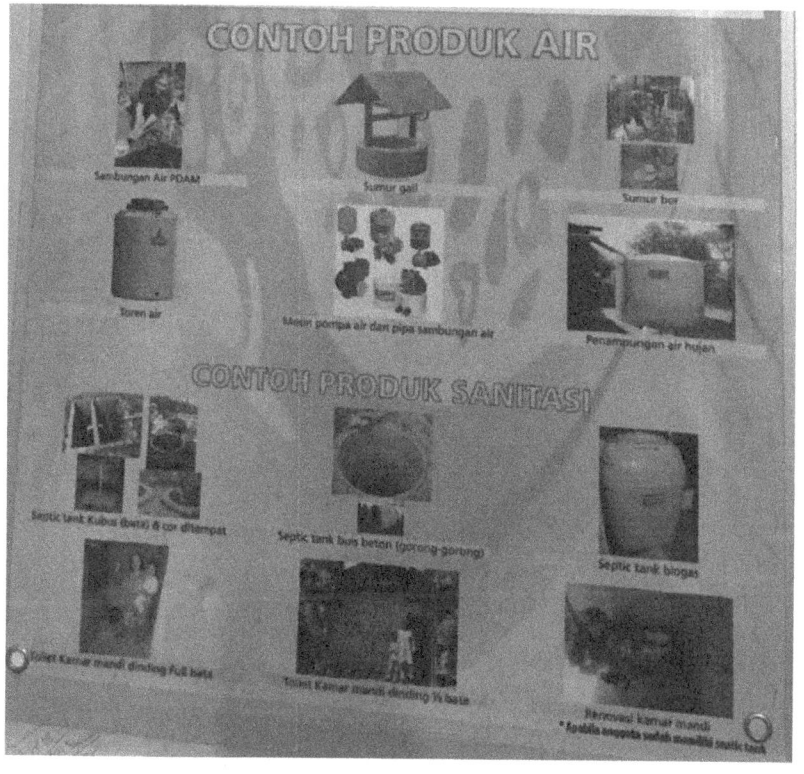

WATER AND SANITATION LOAN OPTIONS AT KOMIDA

WPF has partnered with KOMIDA over three projects to support their business loan. Now in our fourth project together, WPF's board has approved approximately $636,000 USD for scaling up the water/sanitation product at the nine branches that fall under our partnership. The special modifications that KOMIDA made to make the product more affordable for clients means that it brings in less revenue. At the same time, it requires more staff time and effort for promotion and follow up. So, the sanitation product is an expensive undertaking at KOMIDA. Therefore, WPF's free capital subsidizes the cost of funds needed to finance this product.

KOMIDA BORROWER WAHYU WITH HER SON

When KOMIDA members take the sanitation loan, they can apply it depending on water connection availability in their area and their budget. For example, outside a city, it may not be an option to connect to a piped water system. Most clients I visited were investing in a toilet + bathroom + septic tank package.

For example, KOMIDA client, Wahyu, is a member of the Lhong Raya Branch outside Banda Aceh. She has previously borrowed from KOMIDA to finance her sewing/tailor business. She also borrowed 6 million IDR (≈$400) from KOMIDA for a toilet and septic tank which she is repaying in small weekly installments over a two year period. For Wahyu's family, the financing made it possible to build their own toilet. According to KOMIDA's research, now 73% of their members have the ability to have their own toilet with a septic tank.

Chapter 3

Whole Planet Foundation and Microfinance Partners Respond to the COVID-19 Crisis
by Daniel Zoltani

A PHOTO OF MICROCREDIT CLIENTS SHARED BY WPF MICROFINANCE PARTNER IN KENYA, THE BOMA PROJECT

A Message from Whole Planet Foundation's Global Programs Director, Daniel Zoltani

I'm not sure where in the world you're located, but your lifestyle has surely been impacted by what's been happening. Social distancing is the new normal, schools are closing, businesses are closing, and borders are closing. Never in my lifetime has a single threat engulfed the whole world at once. No doubt these are challenging and ever-changing times, and as our Executive Director points out, we are living history.

I want to share with you how microfinance is responding to the COVID-19 pandemic, and its impact on the microentrepreneurs we support through our network of partners on the ground in communities around the globe.

Microfinance clients do not have the luxury of working from home. If their businesses stop, they don't have paid sick leave. As we know well, microcredit has the potential to provide opportunity by jumpstarting or fueling small business, but it does so much more for those living precarious and volatile lives. Access to capital, when provided in a responsible and client-centered way, smooths consumption, offers protection from economic shocks, encourages long-term planning rather than the stress of living day to day, empowers women, and promotes productive investment.

Microfinance in Times of Crisis

Microcredit is a lifeline for our beneficiaries' businesses and thus their livelihoods and it is exactly during times of crisis that it's most important. We have seen this before in West Africa during Ebola, in the Philippines after Super Typhoon Yolanda, the massive 2010 earthquake in Haiti, the earthquake of 2015 in Nepal, typhoons across the Pacific and from countless regional wars and conflicts. In a nutshell, here is what we have learned about disasters from working across 77 countries:

1. As always, poor and marginalized people without access to adequate safety nets are the most at risk.

2. Shocks cause people to fall back into poverty
3. Disasters result in significant loss of livelihood
4. Programming is impacted by disruption of market and supplies chain activities, including closing of local and livestock markets.
5. WPF field partners work in both the immediate response and long-term reconstruction process

Over the years of working with some of the best microfinance organizations around the world, we have observed the following best practices from our microfinance partners during a crisis:

- Prepare relief kits
- Suspend loan repayments
- Offer loan restructuring
- Offer bridge loans
- Offer emergency low-interest loans
- Offer new reconstruction/housing loans
- Link affected clients with relief efforts
- Help transmit public health messages

It's no surprise to me that many of our microfinance partners have already leapt to action in response to COVID-19. Many have taken several steps to safeguard and support their staff and borrowers and to mitigate/minimize risks to the organization. Here are some of the first responses reported:

How our Partners are Responding

The photo at the top of this post shows our Kenya partner BOMA. BOMA has set up a COVID-19 Task Team that has started to communicate best practices on personal hygiene and social distancing to prevent and minimize the spread of COVID-19 virus and instructions on the changes taking place in how BOMA conducts daily business. All international travel, as well as travel between field and regional offices, has been suspended until further notice. All donor and partner visits have been suspended until further notice. In accordance with governments guidelines, the organization has curtailed their program mentorship and monitoring activities by restricting mentors' movements to their own villages/locations. Mentors are instructed to avoid visits to towns, markets and BOMA businesses in densely populated areas. In remote villages, where it is difficult for participants to access information about this pandemic, BOMA mentors, in small group meetings, are sharing Ministry of Health guidance on COVID-19 and conducting training on hygiene and disease prevention.

BOMA's early investment in using technology for program monitoring and management and equipping and training their field staff in the use of tablets, as shown in the photo at the top of this post, is enabling them to quickly adapt to remote work, remote field staff support and management needs. They report,

"Overall, we know that the coming days, weeks, and even months, will pressure test our organization's ability to support both the needs of our staff and participants. However, we feel confident in the great attributes of BOMA as a resilient, adaptive, innovative, results and data driven organization. Our biggest asset, our dedicated board and staff remain healthy, strong and resilient. We are deeply rooted in, and continue to enjoy the support and buy-in from, the communities we work in. We have an incredible base of committed partners, donors and champions. That, we believe, will enable us to successfully navigate any obstacles ahead.

As this pandemic is a fluid situation, we will continue to provide regular updates to you as the situation evolves. We are grateful for your thought and financial partnership and remain committed to our mutual goal of ending extreme poverty in the drylands of Africa."

Our long-standing partner BRAC reports,

"Our teams are coordinating with the Government of Bangladesh, the World Health Organization, and relevant local authorities. Across the entire BRAC family, we are training our staff, as well as community health workers, in hygiene and awareness campaigns so they can educate the broader community about how to minimize health risks while ensuring their own safety. In the camps and settlements of Cox's Bazar [a city in southeastern Bangladesh], our health team is developing public health messages to protect the vulnerable communities that are sheltering there. In all instances, we are working in tandem with and in support of the work of national governments."

In Latin America, our Chilean partner, Fondo Esperanza, is allowing for flexible payments through the end of March and assuring partners that late payments will not affect their account or ability to request future loans. Fundación Paraguaya is promoting repayment through mobile banking and payments that can be done at various convenience stores; offering bank transfers for new/renovated loans and offering hygienic products to those who need them.

Grameen America's Response in the United States
Our partner Grameen America, that operates across 15 U.S. cities, reports that its staff has been equipped with

remote systems and processes to continue the organization's lending program to underserved women entrepreneurs. Grameen America reports:

"Our priority remains working seamlessly as a team to support our branches and our members across the country. Our branch operations across the country have been set up to continue to serve our members during this time of uncertainty, transitioning to implementing remote systems and procedures. Center meetings will be conducted virtually for our borrowers, and disbursements and repayments will continue thanks to the digital technology innovation that has been in effect for several years nationwide."

As the impact on communities continues to escalate, we remain flexible and prepared with contingency plans in every scenario. We remain committed to operating our program and serving our members and their businesses across the country, who need the affordable and available access to capital and community support Grameen America offers.

As Risks Increase for the Poorest, Our Work Continues

While the Whole Planet Foundation team based around the world is grounded, our work is not on hold. We will continue to monitor existing projects, review authorized funding disbursements, and continue communicating with partners as they look to tackle this crisis. We are in the process of designing new processes to do this remotely, and even though we may have to change our approach, we will do all we can to maintain and increase the support we give, especially as the risks increase for the very poorest. It's now more important than ever.

At a time like this we all need to laugh, share, connect, and be together . . . from a safe distance. Please take good care of yourselves and those around you.

DANIEL ZOLTANI (FAR LEFT) PICTURED WITH MEMBERS OF A LOAN GROUP OF WPF MICROFINANCE PARTNER SUPPORT IN BANGLADESH, WITH WPF'S CLAIRE KELLY (SECOND FROM RIGHT)

Chapter 4

COVID-19 and Xenophobia: Reflections from Kenya
by Zoe So

ZOE VISITING ONE OF OUR KENYA PARTNERS, THE BOMA PROJECT

Kenya confirmed a first COVID-19 case on March 13, 2020. The number of known cases has since passed the 200 mark. The country has shut down in phases. I have been mostly self-isolating in my Nairobi home with my husband and in-laws. On video calls with friends and family in New York, Hong Kong, and Kenya, we talk about the usual things in this new normal: The changing economic, social, and travel restrictions in our respective locations. The precautions we're each taking. Our new work-from-home routines, or lack thereof. Our frustrations at that one family member or friend who refuses to take social distancing seriously. What we're watching online. (Me: DNice's Instagram Live DJ sets. Kingdom. Governor Cuomo's daily briefings. And yes, Tiger King.)

A few friends also ask me this: "Are you experiencing any xenophobia?"

I don't really know how to answer this question accurately without going off on a long monologue, so I say simply, "Yes."

In truth, I've only encountered one racist incident overtly related to COVID-19. My husband's family recently opened a café in Nairobi. In the spirit of Hong Kong's ubiquitous 茶餐廳 eateries ("cha chan teng". Translation: tea restaurant), the café has an eclectic fusion menu inspired by our family's roots in Hong Kong, Kenya, and New York. On March 1, someone came to the café to pick up dinner for his boss. I remember it was a balmy evening, typical of Nairobi summer. We had just shifted our hours to stay open a little later, to try to catch the early dinner crowd, and we were glad to see it seemed to be working. As our customer waited for his order, he joked with one of the wait staff, in Kiswahili, "Does the food have coronavirus?" Likely he did not expect that my in-laws and husband, all Kenyan citizens of Chinese descent, could understand him. My husband and father in-law did not respond to the remark directly. Instead, they decided to sit and chat with him in their fluent, Nairobi-accented Kiswahili, building a connection through language.

The unspoken message: "We are Kenyan, just like you."

An off-color joke. No real harm done. Really not that big of a deal, on the spectrum of COVID-19 racism and in the litany of COVID-19 tragedies.

But when I respond "yes," what I really mean is: My in-laws, my husband, and I have been on alert since the first news emerged back in January of a mysterious illness in China, well before the fear and contagion of the virus was immediate in much of the world outside Asia. We talked about avoiding crowded places and markets in case of any violent xenophobic incidents, like this one that took place in Nairobi, and others highlighted in this article. We heard rumors that anyone who looked Chinese was being harassed at the airport, and the nature of my job with Whole Planet Foundation takes me through airports often. We worried whether the café would be affected. When business suddenly took a dip for two weeks in February, well before Nairobians started to self-isolate and the town went quiet, we suspected it was because of fears of the virus. But we could never really know for sure.

I say "yes", because of my own awareness and lived experience of discrimination against Asian-Americans in the United States. Though I know it's unfair to transplant this perspective to Kenyan soil, my conditioned defenses are up. For months, my social media feeds have been filled with Asian-American friends posting with humor and anger and fear about backlash because of the virus. On March 14, in Midland, Texas, a man stabbed members of a Burmese-American family at a Sam's Club out of fear of the disease. Among the victims were two young children, a 2-year-old and a 6-year-old. Physical and verbal assaults persist all over the country, even though the disease itself does not discriminate based on skin color. Anti-Asian sentiment has a long history in the United States, and this pandemic is just the latest trigger. Before COVID-19, there was (and still is) the "yellow peril" rhetoric. Before then, the murder of Vincent Chin, the internment of Japanese Americans during World War II, the Chinese Exclusion Act, and countless other indignities big and small.

Sinophobia in Kenya

The contours of Sinophobia in Kenya are very different. My husband is third generation Chinese Kenyan. His family's chapter in Kenya started during World War II, when my husband's grandfather joined a ship's crew in Hong Kong. When the ship reached Mombasa, on the Kenyan coast, he decided to stay. The family relocated to Nairobi forty years ago. Unlike me, who grew up in New York, my husband did not have the protections and solace of a strong minority community. He can count on his fingers the other Chinese Kenyans of his generation. He personally knows all of them.

In the past five years or so, he has watched as a new surge of immigration has created an increasingly visible Chinese presence in Kenya. This new surge rides on a wave of rapidly growing Chinese investments in infrastructure, many of which come with a large price tag in the form of heavily leveraged government debt. To share a sense of what this shift looks like, I'll borrow a few paragraphs from April Zhu's article in The Elephant, referenced earlier:

"Five years ago, there were only a handful of Chinese restaurants in Nairobi, some Chinese-run casinos and markets, and a dejected "China Centre" that was meant to be doing something diplomatic. Five years ago, there

was no Standard Gauge Railway stretching from Mombasa to Nairobi, built by World Bank-blacklisted Chinese contractors with loans extended by the Chinese Import-Export Bank and tainted with political graft. There was no Xinhua headquarters. No Chinese children at art summer camps. This is no longer the case.

The narrative of the Chinese takeover is a simple story, and simple stories are the strongest, like deep, ready grooves along which individual stories and images slide, all going in the same direction. The Chinese man caning a Kenyan employee melds into frozen Chinese tilapia thawed and sold in Gikomba as Lolwe's fresh catch melds into "Made in China" vitenge melds into the Chinese man caught on video calling Uhuru a monkey."

The ripple effects of the pandemic are adding even more layers to an already complex Africa-China relationship, generating goodwill and anger in rapid succession. As China emerges from their main battle with COVID-19, the government is now contending with the domestic and global reputational fallout of the pandemic while bracing for a potential second wave of the virus.

China has been engaging with countries everywhere through "mask diplomacy." Jack Ma, the co-founder of Chinese tech giant Alibaba, is donating 20,000 test kits, 100,000 masks, and 1,000 PPE units and face shields to each of the 54 countries on the African continent. Kenya and other countries have already received initial shipments. Meanwhile, a cluster of new cases of the virus in China was linked to a Nigerian community in Guangzhou. This past weekend, reports surfaced that Africans in Guangzhou were evicted from their homes, sleeping in the streets, and subjected to forced COVID-

19 testing and quarantine, regardless of travel and contact history. Across Africa, the outcry from the public and backlash from governments have been immediate.

I saw someone from Nairobi post this on Instagram on March 20, re: COVID-19: "If the Chinese come save us we'll be fine. They own half of Kenya so they should!"

A few days ago, as the news of anti-African xenophobia in Guangzhou circulated, a Kenyan Member of Parliament said: "It is only fair that all Chinese nationals leave the country with immediate effect...Go back home."

Versions of this fraught dynamic have been playing out in other countries throughout sub-Saharan Africa since well before COVID-19. Chinese government investments are viewed simultaneously as pragmatic trade-offs, better alternatives to paternalistic "Western" development aid, and a new form of colonialism. In the "takeover narrative," Sinophobia is a reaction of a colonized population against a new colonizing force. The outlines of individual stories disappear, consumed by the bigger narrative. My husband's skin color, and mine, come to symbolize foreignness, privilege, and exploitation.

Closing Thoughts

I have a flow chart of sorts in my head for "responses to racism." (And for sexism too). The decisions pivot mostly on questions of context: Who? Where? Logic and experience tell me that "Where are you really from?," asked repeatedly by an American in New York, probably has a very different subtext than the same question asked by a maize farmer in rural Ethiopia. Context matters. If I'm honest, though, sometimes logic goes out the window and my reactions pivot on my mood: tired, cheeky, irritated, relaxed. Sometimes I snap or pick fights when I shouldn't. I'm not proud of those moments, but they happen.

In the time of COVID-19, it feels like we are all in high gear, striving for logic and calm against a wave of heightened emotions. We balance self-preservation instincts with an inner calling to connect with and help our neighbors. We try to hold on to a sense of normalcy in a world that we suspect is careening out of control, with no end in sight. Almost everyone in the world will be touched by the health, social, and economic tolls of this virus, but we will each experience it in our own ways. This pandemic has exposed some deep cracks in our society. If I can dare to hope for something positive out of all of this, I will hope we come out on the other side of this shared trauma with deeper empathy for each person's unique journey, and a renewed sense of our common humanity.

Chapter 5

Coronavirus is the Latest Dire Challenge Facing Poor Entrepreneurs in Ghana
by Brian Doe

This is a photo of a loan group called Unity Group made up of microentrepreneurs in the poor, northern Accra suburb of Pokuase served by Whole Planet Foundation's Ghanaian microfinance partner ID Ghana.

I visited this group in late January and during the meeting asked the leader of the group about the origin of the group and how it formed. I was surprised to learn that the group actually pre-dates ID Ghana and that the members of this group previously received loans from another local organization which had ceased their ability to carry on lending. Subsequently, Unity Group and many others were transitioned into ID Ghana's portfolio around 2016 to continue receiving training, business loans and savings support from ID Ghana.

MARTIN IS A CLIENT WHO FOUND ID GHANA AFTER ANOTHER MICROLENDING INSTITUTION WENT OUT OF BUSINESS AND STOPPED FINANCING HIS ACTIVITY RENTING AND SELLING CAR BATTERIES

Operating in a Challenging Environment

When we visited ID Ghana this year, it was to check in on how the organization was navigating the challenges facing microfinance institutions in Ghana. Over the past five years over 347 microfinance organizations and 23 microfinance banks have gone under due to a mix of changing government requirements, volatile economic conditions, and a weak finance sector.

However, little did we (or ID Ghana) know that only six weeks after this meeting with Unity Group, the Greater Accra region would be navigating severe restrictions to movement, gatherings and business put in place by the government to prevent the spread of the COVID-19.

The head of ID Ghana, Stephen Dugbazah, reports that as of March 15th all group meetings and trainings with microcredit clients had to be suspended as a result of government restrictions on public gatherings. This has also led to a necessary halt to new loans until the organization can reinstate in-person meetings with their client groups.

MARTIN IS WORKING WITH ID GHANA TO BE ABLE TO IMPROVE THE SITUATION OF HIS BATTERY BUSINESS, WHICH IS CURRENTLY SITTING PRECARIOUSLY OVER A CITY SEWAGE GUTTER, AS SEEN IN THIS PHOTO

SARA IS ID GHANA'S DEDICATED SOCIAL SERVICE COORDINATOR ENSURING THE PROGRAM MEETS ITS GOALS FOR POSITIVE SOCIAL IMPACT ON PARTICIPANTS' LIVES

Building a Strong Foundation with Training and Support

ID Ghana to date has managed to thrive as a high quality, socially-minded business finance program for people living in poverty in a country where inequality is rising and the resources to combat it are increasingly harder to come by. ID Ghana has many strategies to build this strong foundation as a social microfinance organization in Ghana, but it starts with helping their clients to prepare for challenging times. They do this by ensuring all of their members are enrolled in the government health care program, encouraging all participants to save into small savings accounts set up by ID Ghana and requiring them to complete ID Ghana's extensive curriculum of business and financial literacy trainings that staff present with their groups of clients.

During my visit, I witnessed a training titled 'Avoiding Excessive Debt' which aimed to help members of the group understand the causes of being under too much debt and how to avoid getting into a position of excessive debt. This lesson alone prepares microentrepreneurs to build strong foundations for themselves as they grow their small businesses.

With a manageable level of credit and a growing savings account, members can more easily weather difficult periods when revenues drop, rather than go out of business. Under the current restrictions in place against the coronavirus it is likely to be a reality for millions of poor entrepreneurs this year. Whole Planet Foundation continues to monitor the situation with our partners and is proud to support microfinance partners who are focused on serving the poor during uncertain and challenging times.

Whole Planet Foundation has been supporting microentrepreneurs in Ghana since 2010, providing $1.3 million to support over 10,000 microentrepreneurs in both northern and southern Ghana through two microfinance partners as of the writing of this post. WPF began its active partnership with ID Ghana in the southern Greater Accra region in 2017 to help them reach 4,500 new clients with their first business loans through ID Ghana's entry-level loan program for microenterprises and has provided $500,000 in capital to date. ID Ghana's new clients receive on average $155 in capital to start or grow a business activity which is then repaid every two weeks over 6 months. ID Ghana supports a range of microenterprises in the small commerce and services sectors and is working now to receive government permission to expand further into rural areas in other regions in order to launch a planned agriculture finance program.

Chapter 6

From Food Carts to Party Planning, Microbusinesses Weather the Coronavirus Pandemic
by Sandy Mariscal

Businesses around the globe have been disrupted by the 2020 COVID-19 pandemic and are in the spotlight across news channels as the world tries to find its new "normal." Those that are noticeably absent from the daily buzz, yet highly impacted, are microbusinesses run by some of the world's poorest people.

Microcredit clients who receive microloans from Whole Planet Foundation's microfinance partners use their capital to start or develop a variety of different businesses, such as food carts, party planning, childcare and more. Depending on the nature of the microcredit client business, the impacts they are experiencing can range from having to alter their day-to-day business routines if they are deemed essential services, to learning how to incorporate technology to enable social distancing, or just halting their operations completely because of high risk of exposure.

In South America, for instance, some of Whole Planet Foundation's microfinance partners report that approximately half of client businesses are operational, while the other half have come to a screeching halt. The repercussions of these impacts are compounded by the fact that on average, microcredit clients whose loans are funded by Whole Planet Foundation each support an additional 4 people in the family. Microfinance partners supported by Whole Planet Foundation are pivoting quickly to support clients through this crisis by implementing tactics, such as loan repayment grace periods, introduction of digital solutions and more frequent check-ins with clients. These efforts are aimed to help clients stay afloat so they can continue to provide their services to their communities.

An Introduction to Microcredit in Peru

My first experience meeting a microcredit client was during a trip to Peru on the Whole Foods Market Team Member Volunteer Program in 2011. I was lucky to travel to a country where Whole Foods Market sourced products to witness the power of microcredit. I embarked on this journey with several questions. How does microcredit work? Who are we supporting with funds raised in Whole Foods Market stores? What types of businesses are the clients starting out of their homes?

SANDY AND WHOLE FOODS MARKET TEAM MEMBERS VOLUNTEERING AT AN
ELEMENTARY SCHOOL IN AREQUIPA, PERU

279

My visit to Pro Mujer, Whole Planet Foundation's microfinance partner in Arequipa, Peru, allowed me the opportunity to meet microfinance staff and learn about Pro Mujer's operations. But the highlight of that day? Meeting microcredit clients for the first time! Our group was excited to meet the women we heard were doing such wonderful things with the loans we helped fund. The first encounter played out perfectly. We walked into a larger room to find a group of women who stood to welcome us.

For a split-second there was complete silence, then cameras flashed on both sides of the room, and that caused everyone to burst into laughter. It seems anticipation was felt by both groups, as the women shared that they too had were just as eager to meet the donors that had help fund their loans. In the time of handshakes and hugs, we greeted each other and began our learning journey as we sat to listen to their stories and learn about their many businesses. From childcare to food service to clothing stores, the types of businesses varied widely as the women leveraged their passions and talents to launch their income generating ventures.

SANDY AND WHOLE FOODS MARKET TEAM MEMBERS AT PRO MUJER IN AREQUIPA, PERU

Microcredit Client Businesses in the USA

The experience was profound and inspired me to continue supporting Whole Planet Foundation when I arrived back home. I continued to fundraise and shared my experience to raise awareness of the mission. In 2015, I was delighted to join the Whole Planet Foundation team and my passion project became my passion career.

Throughout my five years at Whole Planet Foundation, I continued to visit our client businesses as I led donor impact visits to our US projects. These trips allow generous partners the opportunity to learn about Whole Planet Foundation's microfinance partner's operations, visit microcredit client businesses and witness their donated dollars at work. Currently, Whole Planet Foundation works in 19 cities across the United States. Below are some of the stories, I collected at the many businesses we visited.

Guadalupe's Story: A Restaurant in Jackson Heights

Guadalupe is a microcredit client of one of Whole Planet Foundation's microfinance partner in the United States, Grameen America In Jackson Heights, Queens, New York. Guadalupe loves cooking traditional Mexican food. Her friends always told her she should start a business to share her talent of cooking delicious foods with others. Finding the capital to support this dream wasn't easy.

Fortunately, she was introduced to financial services provided by Grameen America. With the help of microcredit, Guadalupe was able to start a bustling Mexican restaurant in the heart of her community in Jackson Heights. Bella Puebla Mexican Restaurant serves unique and traditional dishes from Mexico. Guadalupe has used additional microloans to expand her business and purchase equipment and inventory. Bella Puebla is noted for having one of the most extensive menus in the city, and the sophisticated kitchen has been written up in well-known publications for its delicious and authentic cuisine.

Guadalupe is thrilled that she has been able to achieve her dream. She shared that the women who participate in Grameen America's microlending program are hard working women who just want to be given a chance. She is grateful for that opportunity, as it has empowered her to take control of her future and share her passion for cooking with others.

GUADALUPE AT HER RESTAURANT IN QUEENS, NEW YORK

Ledy's Story: Entrepreneurship for Generations

Ledy is a microcredit client of Grameen America in Oakland, California. She has been a saleswoman all her life, starting with the sale of crafts in Ecuador. Her mother is also a saleswoman who had started a small craft stand in the Fruitvale District in Oakland. When her mother grew seriously ill, Ledy took over the small business to support the family. In order to grow the business and expand her inventory, Ledy reached out to Grameen America for access to capital. With her first loan, she purchased additional goods that she heard would sell well in her community.

LEDY AND HER MOTHER AT THEIR MARKET STAND IN OAKLAND, CALIFORNIA

Since 2012, she had received 10 microloans from Grameen America and had borrowed over $40,000. Every loan was put to good use and repaid. She utilized the funds to help her establish a storefront and buy additional merchandise from Latin America. She now sells crafts, clothing and accessories at the farmers market and out of her small store in the Fruitvale District. In response to customer traffic, she alternates her days between her store and the farmers market to make her products available to new customers traveling via the Bart public transportation system which is close to the market. She also has been savvy with savings. Knowing that business during the winter season is slower, she saves more in the summer to keep the business going during slower winter months. Ledy shared that the opportunity to grow her business and the support she receives from other women in her microcredit group, has helped her support her family.

Commonalities of hardship and perseverance across the many microcredit client narratives Whole Planet Foundation collects and shares, like Guadalupe's and Ledy's stories, demonstrate that these women are no strangers to adversity.

While microcredit clients now strive against additional obstacles caused by the coronavirus pandemic, they will undoubtedly be determined to work through those new challenges to continue to monetize their various talents in support of their families.

Whole Planet Foundation and its microfinance partners are dedicated to supporting their efforts by strategizing how to best continue to provide access to capital and shift operations to best support microentrepreneurs as they weather these difficult times. By sharing information and best practices and listening to the valuable feedback clients offer, we'll pivot together to continue to further our collective mission of financial inclusion and poverty alleviation. Small businesses are vital to our economy and the livelihood of many families, so we must do our part to ensure microentrepreneurship is not stifled by the known and unknown challenges ahead.

Chapter 7

The Pledge to Protect Microfinance Institutions and their Clients from the Economic Effects of COVID-19

By Brian Doe

At the start of the COVID-19 pandemic in 2020, Whole Planet Foundation signed on to the *Key Principles to Protect Microfinance Institutions and their Clients in the COVID-19 Crisis*, supporting dialogue and collective action to help microfinance institutions support their clients in this difficult period. WPF has been following and is supportive of other similar efforts including the *MOU on Coordination among MIVs in response to Covid 19* launched in April 2020.

As shown in the photo above, WPF's microfinance partner Sampurna Training and Entrepreneurship Programme (STEP) in India restarted their activities in June in full force. STEP has provided health trainings about COVID to almost 10,000 borrowers and distributed 1,000 masks as of the writing of this postt.

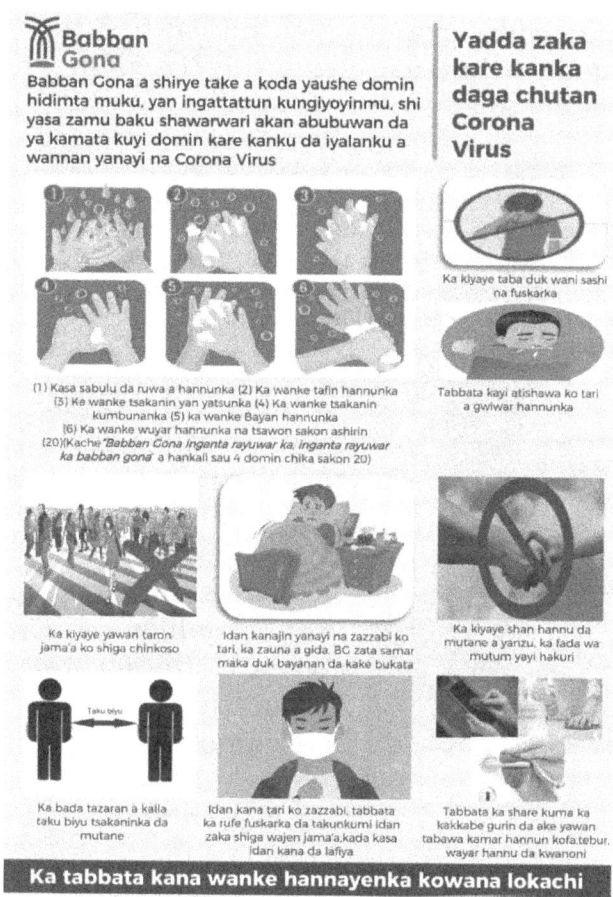

IN NIGERIA, WPF PARTNER BABBAN GONA HAS CIRCULATED POSTERS AS PART OF THEIR COVID-19 AWARENESS CAMPAIGN IN AREAS OF OPERATION.

As members of Whole Planet Foundation's Programs team, for the last two months we have been focusing on close and careful communication with our microfinance partners as they navigate an unprecedented shutdown of their local markets, due to restrictions intended to combat the spread of COVID-19. This shutdown is preventing their clients from doing business, which means those entrepreneur clients are struggling to make a living and will certainly face difficulties repaying the business loans that are ordinarily used to grow their business activities.

WPF PARTNER CAURIE IN SENEGAL FACES OBSTACLES OWING TO COVID RESTRICTIONS AND THEIR FOCUS ON RURAL LARGE GROUP LOANS. HOWEVER, THE SHUTDOWNS HAVE HAD THE POSITIVE IMPACT OF ACCELERATING THE DEVELOPMENT OF THEIR MOBILE WALLET FEATURE THAT WILL INCREASE REMOTE TRANSACTIONS FOR CLIENTS

WPF receives its funds as donations which permits us to offer microfinance institutions free capital and a degree of flexibility on repaying capital in situations where clients are unexpectedly unable to run their businesses. However, this isn't the case with most supporters and investors in the microfinance industry. The large majority of capital that enables microfinance comes in the form of external loans that are repaid by microfinance institutions on a regular basis with varying levels of interest.

Over the course of this crisis, WPF has been heartened to see many types of investors from the microfinance sector coming together to make commitments to ensure microfinance institutions are able to keep their capital in place until the COVID-19 crisis subsides and local businesses restart, even if that capital was meant to be repaid to investors in 2020. The crisis is also sparking collective conversations between microfinance investors on how they will address a future economic crisis started by COVID-19 which could continue to deteriorate economies in poor communities after lockdowns are lifted.

WPF joined the Pledge of Key Principles (see more at the bottom of this post) aiming to help build momentum for a toolbox that diverse types of investors can use to collectively help microfinance institutions survive this crisis and be well placed to quickly help client businesses once COVID-19 lockdowns end. WPF was impressed with the social focus of the Pledge and its first objective to create an open dialogue between lenders to collectively work to ensure capital stays with the microfinance institutions that all are seeking to support.

Some of the unique tools that WPF found particularly important in this Pledge among microfinance investors include:

- A clear statement that the objective of collective action is ultimately to help entrepreneurs survive the consequences of COVID-19 and that while investors need to ensure capital stays with microfinance institutions this flexibility should positively impact the entrepreneurs that are suffering by ensuring that these clients are not aggressively pressured to repay loans amidst overwhelmingly difficult economic conditions;

- A united front to minimize requests for information by collectively creating common reporting formats that can be used to facilitate the dialogue between lenders and institutions to ensure microfinance institutions are devoting their time to addressing client needs and not responding to endless lender queries;

- Thinking ahead now on how to limit the impact of future deterioration in the global economy sparked by COVID-19 which can result, for example, from fast deterioration of local currency values that would make investments in U.S. dollars or other currencies extremely difficult to repay. This pledge builds on important lessons learned from the 2008 financial crisis on how to quickly mobilize to collectively restructure overall debt owed by microfinance institutions if COVID-19's impact becomes a long-term crisis for entrepreneur clients.

STEP HAS ALWAYS FOCUSED ON VOCATIONAL AND ENTREPRENEURSHIP TRAINING ALONGSIDE THEIR FINANCIAL SERVICES. THEY HAVE JUST LAUNCHED A NEW PROGRAM TO SUPPORT 25 WOMEN WITH MASK MAKING. THE STEP ENTREPRENEURS WILL SELL THE MASKS IN THE LOCAL MARKET AND STEP WILL MAKE ORDERS DIRECTLY FROM THEM AS WELL.

As a charitable foundation that prioritzes a social return on its investments in microfinance (the alleviation of poverty through access to fair financial services) more than a monetary return, WPF is now asking how the sector that funds microfinance could go further while understanding the constraints faced by other lenders.

We are fortunate that with the support of Whole Foods Market, Whole Planet Foundation's program staff have the opportunity to visit every active partnership annually, which has allowed the Foundation to build a nuanced perspective of how these institutions operate and their unique vulnerabilities. With this in-depth perspective, WPF wants to turn to the larger circle of investors and supporters to ask that the following considerations are also brought into collective conversations initiated by this pledge of Key Principles:

- If your institution can delay or forgive interest to a microfinance institution, can that institution be empowered to in turn delay or forgive the interest owed by their clients? Or might it allow the institution to retain staff that can help ensure the viability of that institution?: Every investor in microfinance is bound by the constraints imposed by their sources of capital, but WPF wants to ensure there is also transparency in lenders' ability to delay or forgive the cost of that capital through interest and fees that microfinance institutions often pay but may not be covered by revenues coming in from microlending activities when business activities stop during a crisis.

- Can this pledge be the start of a roadmap for increasing capacity and planning before the next crisis hits? And can this pledge be the starting point for on-going collective planning to protect the microfinance sector? The pledge on Key Principles calls for increased technical assistance for microfinance institutions struggling to manage a fast-paced crisis, but how many institutions can quickly mobilize technical experts in the midst of a fast-moving crisis while also managing requests for updates from a wide range of lenders? The lender community can help to build a more resilient system by going further than contractual covenants to include crisis management, preparedness training and capacity building with microfinance institutions over the course of an investment.

During the collective action discussion, WPF hopes lenders will tailor their responses for those institutions that go furthest to serve vulnerable communities in need but may face bigger challenges to survival than more commercially successful microfinance institutions: WPF supports microfinance institutions that bring their clients a wide range of extra services that other financial service providers don't offer. This often comes with the trade-offs of lower cash reserves, thinner operating margins and a more vulnerable clientele. In ordinary times, WPF sees these partners roll out trainings in villages, support health services, work with remote community-based savings groups and offer doorstep delivery of quality agricultural inputs to small-scale farmers.

These same institutions, over the course of the COVID-19 crisis, have translated health information into local languages, delivered sanitation supplies across wide areas, offered crisis grants to clients that have lost their business capital and diverted their institutional equity to cover staff salaries while lending stopped due to COVID-19. These institutions are usually registered as non-profit organizations and may be registered as local cooperatives or credit unions that place maximum resources to create social impact and lower costs to poor clients. These institutions may not have the biggest loan portfolios, but rather the greatest depth in serving poor borrowers in remote or marginalized areas.

WPF has been supporting microfinance institutions since 2006 with a mix of grant capital and no-interest loans across 77 countries and is preparing not only for the aftermath of the COVID-19 crisis but also the eventuality of other future long-term external shocks that are sure to bring further challenges to micro, small and medium-sized businesses in poor communities. Whole Planet Foundation looks forward to continuing the conversation with other supporters and investors in the sector to work towards a sustainability plan for ensuring the long-term viability of pro-poor microfinance globally.

More about the Pledge

In response to the health and economic crisis caused by COVID-19, a group of lenders, platforms and key players of the inclusive financial sector committed to a common pledge: *"Key principles to protect microfinance institutions and their clients in the Covid-19 crisis"*. Initiated by the Grameen Crédit Agricole Foundation, this pledge was built in consensus between all original signatories. The objective is to protect both the microfinance institutions and their clients to ensure the continued access to funding in the best possible conditions and to look out for clients' and staff well-being.

The pledge aims to guide stakeholders to better support microfinance institutions and vulnerable clients during this crisis. The main principles of the pledge are the pooling of available information, analyses and anticipations, as well as the concerted implementation of shared decisions. The signatories agree to coordinate policies, technical assistance and resources to help microfinance institutions in this unprecedented crisis.

Since its publication in May, five new organizations have signed the pledge. This initiative now counts 26 signatories active in Africa, Asia, Eastern Europe and Latin America: ADA, Alterfin, Azerbaijan Micro-finance Association, Bamboo Capital Partners, Cerise, CIDR Pamiga, Cordaid Investment Management, Crédit Agricole CIB India, CA Indosuez Wealth (Asset Management), Crédit Agricole S.A., European Microfinance Network, FS Impact Finance, GAWA Capital, Grameen Crédit Agricole Foundation, InFiNe.lu, Inpulse, Kiva, Luxembourg Microfinance And Development Fund, MCE Social Capital, Microfinance African Institutions Network, Microfinance Centre, Rabo Foundation, SIDI, SIMA, Social Performance Task Force and Whole Planet Foundation.

The signatories welcome additional stakeholders to join this common initiative. The coordination of efforts to support microfinance institutions' actions is essential to overcome this crisis.

Part VIII

WHOLE PLANET FOUNDATION TEAM MEMBER STORIES & GUEST BLOGS

Chapter 1

Spotlight on our Global Programs Director Daniel Zoltani

DANIEL WITH A MICROCREDIT CLIENT IN MYANMAR

What in your education, life experience, and professional background led you to this job?

I had the fortunate opportunity to study abroad, and was introduced to the concept of microcredit in an economic development course. I completed a semester in Valparaiso, Chile and a semester in Buenos Aires, Argentina. At this point I was struck by the bug and there was no turning back. Upon graduating from the University of Colorado with degrees in Economics and International Affairs, I wanted to continue to explore the world; in part because of a growing wandering spirit but also a drive to live life through experience. I figured a bike ride through Central America would be a great place to start.

Through this journey, I connected with hardworking farmers, diverse rural commerce and talented artisans working to make ends meet. I picked up Muhammad Yunus' book "Banker to The Poor" and serendipitously crossed paths with an organization that was helping these women start and grow their businesses. It was called Grameen Guatemala, the microfinance organization started by Grameen Trust and Whole Planet Foundation two years earlier. Quickly my plan for a 3-month bike trip through Central America turned into a 3-year long assignment supporting the expansion of Grameen from Guatemala to Mexico to Colombia. From Latin America, I was recruited by Whole Planet Foundation and would spend the next five years living and working in Asia managing our growing Asia/Pacific portfolio before assuming the role of Global Programs Director in December 2015.

What's your favorite part of the job?

Collectively, our small field team based around the world has enormous access to a diverse group of microfinance organizations implementing a diverse set of financial inclusion models. I enjoy and appreciate the unique access we are granted. Whether this is speaking with the organization's board of directors to better understand overall strategy or the organizations management to discuss business and outreach plans, or the field staff to review different methodologies in serving the poorest or speaking with the clients to discuss what they see as their challenges and opportunities. The job is an ongoing learning experience!

DANIEL WITH ZOE, REGIONAL DIRECTOR FOR EAST/SOUTH AFRICA, IN UGANDA VISITING PARTNER VILLAGE ENTERPRISE AND COLLECTING LOCAL RECIPES FOR THE WPF COOKBOOK

What's the most interesting thing you have learned on the job in the last month?

In the last month I visited existing and potential new partners in Cambodia, Nepal and India with Claire Kelly our Asia/Pacific Regional Director. In addition to visiting traditional microfinance organizations, we also visited four non-traditional microfinance social enterprises. In India and Nepal the organizations were providing

297

financing for home solar kits and last mile distribution of consumer products like diapers, sanitary pads, and life enhancing kitchen appliances. In Cambodia, one organization was providing financing for water filters, while the other was providing agriculture inputs on credit. Often the social enterprise model can provide additional value added to the clients beyond financing, such as access to high quality productive assets and access to markets.

We took the strategy of comparing the social enterprise products and services with our existing MFI partner in Cambodia, Chamroeun. In our analysis – we found the agriculture financing services offered through the social enterprise were superior to the agriculture financing products offered at Chamroeun. While Chamroeun does provide modified agriculture repayment schedules with grace periods, they do not provide access to inputs, agriculture training or market buybacks. On the other hand, Chamroeun was offering water filters at a competitive price and with 12-month financing bundled with a business loan. So regarding the water filters, the Chamroeun approach was more aligned with our traditional model and client centric in terms of product choice and accessibility. Based on this comparison, we are now taking additional steps to further explore a potential partnership with the agriculture financing organization.

Tell a story of the microcredit client or MFI partner colleague who has inspired you the most.

I would like to share about Moslima, a client of BRAC Bangladesh's UltraPoor/Graduation program. Moslima chose a milk cow for her enterprise activity.

298

In the Ultra Poor program, rather than a loan, an initial asset is granted as part of the one-time intervention for the very poorest. Moslima expects the cow will produce 2-3 liters a day, so she can keep one liter and sell the remainder for approximately 40 taka/liter ($0.50).

She has no plans to sell the cow, but wants to take care of it and raise a couple of calves which she can eventually sell. Until the cow starts to produce milk, Moslima sells the cow dung to neighbors for fuel. This is her first income generating activity. Her modest home, a mud hut with a tin roof, has two rooms. One for her and her family and the other for her new cow that she proudly named White Babou – roughly translated as "elegance."

MOSLIMA WILL USE THE PROFITS FROM HER COW, WHICH SHE'S NAMED
WHITE BABOU, TO CONTINUE HER PATH OUT OF POVERTY

At WPF we believe entrepreneurs are everywhere—but they are not defined by occupation, gender, age, or income. What makes them an entrepreneur is their perseverance and tenacious spirit to improve their lives and the lives of their family.

What do you like to do when you're not working?

While I spend a LOT of my time traveling internationally for work, I am a homebody when in Austin. I find peace in home projects, and gardening and have recently discovered a passion for masonry, beekeeping and sailing.

DANIEL ADMIRES A PIZZA BAKING IN THE WOOD-FIRED OVEN HE BUILT IN HIS BACKYARD IN AUSTIN, TEXAS

Chapter 2

Spotlight on WPF's "The Wizard" Victor Quiroz

WPF'S VICTOR QUIROZ ON A VISIT TO INDIA

What in your education, life experience, and professional background led you to this job?

I graduated from St. Edward's University in Austin, TX with a B.A. in Business Administration. While in school I interned as a Grant Writer working with the BeeHive of Austin, a nonprofit that provides after-school programming for at-risk youth. I also interned as a Risk Analyst with Rêv Worldwide, a company that promotes financial inclusion by providing pre-paid payment solutions. I joined Whole Planet Foundation as a Program Analyst Intern in February 2012. At the time, I was brought on to help organize how the Programs Team collects data and to build management tools around the data. Six months later it turned into a full-time role.

VICTOR (LEFT) WITH A FIELD CREDIT OFFICER VISITING MICROCREDIT CLIENTS OF WPF PARTNER UMUTANGUHA FINANCE COMPANY IN RWANDA IN 2018

What's your favorite part of the job?

In my role, I get to live in our data and get to continuously explore new ways to improve our systems. I enjoy the challenge of learning how to use new tools and building solutions that help support our team. However, my favorite part is getting to work with a great team.

What's the most interesting thing you have learned on the job in the last month?

I have gotten to work with the Whole Foods Market Data Visualization Team to build a Tableau dashboard for our upcoming Prosperity Campaign. I'd played with the software here and there [in the past], but now I am blown away by the functionality that it has to offer. With their help we have a new tool that effectively communicates our fundraising initiatives during the campaign.

Tell a story of the microcredit client or MFI partner colleague who has inspired you the most.

While traveling in India, we met a client named Kiran who was on her second microloan with CASHPOR and was raising livestock. This memory sticks with me because Kiran was very confident and excited to share with us her experience working with CASHPOR.

A PHOTOGRAPH OF KIRAN, A MICROCREDIT CLIENT IN INDIA

Kiran had borrowed 30,000 INR ($465) this cycle, compared to 15,000 INR ($233) her first cycle. She used the capital to buy two goats and one cow. Since the investment, six baby goats had been born! Kiran told me each goat can produce about ½ liter of milk per day which she could sell. She could also sell the goats for goat meat after 8-15 months for around 3-4000 INR ($47-62). Previously, Kiran had grown rice, so animal husbandry diversified her income.

What do you like to do when you're not working?

When I'm not working, I enjoy getting out and exploring. My wife Natalie and I regularly take our two dogs out wherever we can and we enjoy traveling and getting to enjoy new experiences. We also enjoy going to see concerts and check out new places that have opened in our neighborhood.

VICTOR AND HIS WIFE NATALIE VISITING GUANAJUATO IN 2017

Chapter 3

Field Notes from Paraguay:
From a Whole Foods Market Team Member Volunteer
By Adelle Housker

"When it's really hot, that sometimes happens," said our guide, Maria del Mar. The lights and air conditioning died while we were eating lunch at a restaurant called La Vienes in the San Lorenzo strip mall where our community liaison, Nelson Garay, was buying additional supplies for the yurt construction at Ferrex (essentially, the Paraguayan Home Depot).

It was wintertime in the southern hemisphere. Maria explained that she runs a race every year at this time when it's usually "so cold, ten degrees Celsius." (A fellow volunteer, Sal, translated, "Fifty-ish degrees Fahrenheit.") However, from the news popping up on Maria's phone – participants perishing from heat stroke – it wasn't hard to believe that so far, it was the hottest day of the trip: 107 degrees Fahrenheit.

Luckily that particular Sunday we were in the air-conditioned van, travelling from the capital Asunción – where we'd spent the first half of the Whole Foods Market Team Member Volunteer Program – to Curuguaty, a city on the edge of the Mbaracayú Reservation, where we commuted every day during our stay with the Aché Tribe.

The flat palm savannah gave way to heavily forested hills, the incline of which proved a little too much for the van, which began to smell of burnt tires. Marco, our Discover South America guide, slid open the doors. Utter silence filled the back. He cheerfully explained that we got an opportunity to stretch while our driver Cesar would be checking the water level of the radiator.

TEAM MEMBER VOLUNTEERS WITH CHILDREN IN THE ACHÉ COMMUNITY

306

We had no choice but to hope for the best. Walking on the shoulder, slowly ambling as motorcycles sped past, a fellow volunteer, Jill, exclaimed, "Uff da!"

"Jill, where did you learn that word? I haven't heard that word in years!" I exclaimed, having left my hometown in the Midwest over two years ago.

"From my days in Minnesota," she explained.

Marco pointed out the Cordillera Hills. We passed a large white cross, and he explained that pilgrims make the ten-kilometer trek from the base of the hill to this cross every December. He also mentioned that these pilgrimages take place at night because of the heat.

We got back to the van, relieved to find that were not stranded, and continued on as planned to our destination. Between Carlos in the driver seat and Marco in the passenger seat, was wedged a *guampa* (gourd cup) and *bombilla* (straw). Inside this cup was a kind of tea – yerba mate. It was this tea that was responsible for bringing eight Whole Foods Market Team Members to the middle of this vibrant, incredible country on an adventure that would change our lives.

Though they speak Guaraní, the Aché are not ethnically Guaraní. After a half-century of dealing with encroaching developers and illegal loggers, the Aché were finally permitted to resettle the land in 2003, and Guayakí partnered with the hunter-gatherers to help them learn a new skill: crop cultivation. With this skill, they have been able to turn a profit from the jungle they wished to preserve. The Aché Food Sovereignty Project supported by Guayakí provides food to the community and a supply of yerba mate, the caffeinated plant Guayakí purchases from the Aché to export to U.S. retailers like Whole Foods Market.

Yerba Mate is a tree belonging to the holly family, and because of its three xanthines – not only caffeine, but theobromine and theophylline – it is prized for the sustained energy an infusion of its leaves provides. Its seeds become viable after passing through the digestive tract of birds like toucans, and so it was difficult for the Jesuit missionaries to find a way to cultivate it in the 17th century. However, they eventually discovered that a germination period of a full nine months of continually moistening the seed would do the trick. The plant grows beneath the canopy of sub-tropical jungles.

Though they can be grown in plantations under direct sunlight, Alex Pryor (the co-founder of Guayakí, whom we met and who was on the scaffolding sweating under the intense sun and drinking the mate along with the rest of us volunteers) was expressly against such cultivation techniques. Having grown up drinking the beverage in Argentina, he got the idea for introducing the drink to the United States when he came to California to study, and found a sun-kissed culture that would be "perfect" for it.

During our visit, we were allowed to plant yerba mate saplings in dirt gathered from the forest floor. Volunteers pressed the delicate little plants into small bags, rousing up a friendly competition for who could plant the most the fastest. Scooping up the cool dirt with our hands, we chatted excitedly about – for example – the exoskeleton we'd found in the soil, our impressions of the cute toddlers that would come up to hug us, the three University students and Guayakí teams from Argentina and Brazil who had come to join us, or the surprising speed with which we (none of us being carpenters or particularly handy) had managed to build a yurt.

With the help of Milo Demandre, a volunteer from Patagonia, and the Aché themselves, we built the yurt that was to serve as a Montessori school for the tribe's younger members in just three days. The construction of the yurt was a perfect example of Guayakí's relationship with the Aché. The idea to build a yurt and train teachers so that younger children of the tribe might have access to education came from a series of dialogues between Guayakí and the Aché, an open-minded give-and-take that is characteristic of Alex's brand of collaboration.

We gathered the bags of saplings into the nursery, under a green mesh canopy stretched across wooden posts and fenced off to protect from pests. Later, we went on a walk through the jungle. As they went, children from the tribe picked off huge leaves the size of a grown man's torso, and fashioned them into hats which they crowned us with. Nelson Garay pointed out the mature yerba mate trees they'd planted. The university students (one of whom was Nelson's son) delicately unwound any vines from their trucks with machetes. We made a stop at a watering hole. The children jumped in from the high muddy banks, and the rest of us cooled off, pressing the water against our foreheads and necks.

Later, we met Alex's parents, who drove up to participate in the tour and meet with this cheerful gathering. His father discussed an array of topics from ecology to history; and his mother, who oversaw the training of the Aché's Montessori teachers, gave a detailed and fascinating account of the background context. They were refined, dressed in white linen and wide-brimmed hats. Though roughly my grandparents' age, they had no qualms about joining us in the rainforest. We were to meet several characters like that throughout our brief two weeks in Paraguay – larger than life.

Chapter 4

Whole Foods Market Team Member Volunteer Program Introduces Team Members to Global Communities

By Genie Bolduc

TEAM MEMBER VOLUNTEERS MEET MICROCREDIT CLIENTS OF
ENTREPRENEURS DU MONDE/ASSILASSIME IN TOGO

Whole Planet Foundation was founded in 2005. Since 2007, over 850 Whole Foods Market Team Members have been to communities around the world to witness the transformative power of microcredit through the Whole Foods Market Team Member Volunteer Program. Team Members apply, pay for their plane tickets and immunizations, and volunteer their time for this 2 week program.

Whole Foods Market covers in-country travel, accommodations, meals, guides, and the budget for the community service projects in which the volunteers participate.

From building water wells and refurbishing schools in Madagascar, to building a water tower and repairing irrigation channels in the high Atlas Mountains of Morocco, to building 3 new classrooms and refurbishing a school in Honduras, to building playgrounds and water catchment tanks in the Thar Desert of India, Team Members get to make a real difference in these rural communities and carry the relationships that they form with community members and each other with them for the rest of their lives.

TEAM MEMBER VOLUNTEERS PLANTING TREES IN PARAGUAY

Teams have traveled to Brazil, Colombia, Costa Rica, Ghana, Guatemala, India, Kenya, Madagascar, Morocco, Nepal, Paraguay, Peru, South Africa, Thailand, Togo, and the United States since 2007. Team Member Volunteers witness many difficult things: extreme poverty, need and the often intense struggle to prosper in rural communities.

The core experience that drives the popularity and the deep impact of the Whole Foods Market Team Member Volunteer Program is the opportunity to meet recipients of the microloans that Whole Planet Foundation has funded through local microlending partners. To meet these women, to see their small, often home-based businesses, and to get to hear them share their challenges and successes, turns a Team Member from a supporter of Whole Planet Foundation and the transformative power of microcredit, into a true ambassador.

To see in person how microfinance works on a day-to-day basis, to see how hard the microfinance staff of WPF's partners works to serve their community members, and to hear personal stories from the microlending staff and the microloan recipients themselves, changes the way the Team Members think about microcredit. It inspires them and instills in them the deepest desire to share what they have learned with their fellow Team Members and Whole Foods Market shoppers. In turn, they then inspire their team and WFM shoppers to action, getting involved in helping people at home and around the world with the opportunity of prosperity through access to microcredit.

Chapter 5

Whole Foods Market Team Member Volunteer Program Trip to Togo: An Opportunity to See Microcredit in Action

By Jason Martinez

The Whole Foods Market Team Member Volunteer Program is an incredible opportunity that Whole Foods Market offers its Team Members that allow them to visit a foreign country where Whole Planet Foundation supports microcredit. The trips are typically around two weeks long where Team Members are submerged into the local culture, learning how Whole Planet Foundation works with microfinance institutions to alleviate poverty in that particular country.

I had the opportunity to visit Togo, Africa, and I chose Togo because it was the country that I knew the least about and is relatively unknown to most people I know. Togo is a small country in West Africa sandwiched between Ghana and Benin, and there is very little tourist infrastructure. Team Members are typically hosted by Whole Foods Market suppliers, and longtime supporter of Whole Planet Foundation, Alaffia hosted our group. Their mission aims to alleviate poverty and advance gender equality through the Fair Trade of indigenous resources and community empowerment projects and aligns well with what Whole Planet Foundation does.

Our experience with microcredit began bright and early the day after we arrived as we got to meet with representatives from Whole Planet Foundation Microfinance Partner Entrepreneurs du Monde. Entrepreneurs du Monde has a program in Togo that goes by Assilassimé Solidarité (hand in hand) that is used to provide microfinance in the country. They taught us about the methodology and processes that they use in Togo to identify and select microcredit clients. At the time, their portfolio was made up of 5204 active borrowers, with 98% of them being women entrepreneurs. The average first loan was the equivalent of $71USD, and they had a 95% repayment rate.

After learning about their methodology, we had the opportunity to visit a few clients and learn first-hand how they support their clientele and how their clientele support each other. We first visited Mama, who runs a small fruit and vegetable stand in a local market. Before receiving a loan, she used to carry a basket of fruit around the market trying to sell it. The loan allowed her to obtain a stand in the market and buy additional inventory to sell. We learned how small loans can have a large impact helping clients create a sustainable business.

Next we learned how the repayment process works by observing and participating in one of the monthly group repayment meetings. We learned how the group dynamic is instrumental in the success of clients, especially those first starting out. These groups create a community of support where clients can discuss issues and receive training on several topics such as the importance of saving money or how diversification can lead to growth. While payments are being reconciled there is always time for fun and entertainment!

Finally, we had lunch at small restaurant owned by Nasoma, a client who had been working with Assiliasimé for a while. She had grown her business into a small corner store and restaurant. We enjoyed a delicious meal and learned of her plans to expand into a form of catering.

Being able to meet microcredit clients, contribute to their businesses, and being part of a group meeting was an unforgettable experience. It's one thing to hear about or read about microcredit, but the Team Member Volunteer Program allows Team Members to participate in the actual process and meet the very lives that are being empowered.

Chapter 6

Whole Foods Market Team Member Volunteer Program Trip to Guatemala

By Sarah Tack

My name is Sarah Tack. I'm the Culture Champion Ambassador for Whole Foods Market.

I had the pleasure of being able to participate in the first Whole Foods Market Volunteer Program with Whole Planet Foundation in 2007, in a small village near Lake Atitlan in the Guatemalan highlands of the Sierra Madre Mountain range. The trip was, and continues to be even 13 years later, transformative.

The beauty of the experience that you have volunteering is the complete and total vulnerability that you experience. I can still remember right when I got off the plane, how Guatemala smelled, the excitement and nervousness that extended to every part of my being as we wound through the mountains in the dark to my hotel, my insecurities in my broken Spanish and meeting Team Members that had done so much from all over the company for the first time. Over and over again I was cracked open by the total unfamiliarity of my surroundings, and Guatemala, and the people that I met there, welcomed me with support, love, curiosity and shared experience.

The people that we met through the social works projects that we participated in, or from the group of microfinance recipients that the Whole Planet Foundation was working with through Grameen Trust, or just the people that we met through living in a new town, in a shared home; all of these people were warm, welcoming, open and curious, just like me.

Not only did I get to see how differently people in other parts of the world live, but more importantly, I got to see how much we shared in our human experience.

I got to see how my fellow Team Members experienced life in their parts of the country, and how the people that lived in Guatemala experienced their lives in the villages we were living in, and was surprised to see how much commonality there was for all of us. There was so much more that I found familiar than different in all of the people I met.

It created a sense of ease and connection that I have carried with me since that time. It also continues to fuel me and contribute to my growth as I go through new experiences in my life. I often say that I would not be the kind of mother that I am had I have not had the opportunity to volunteer, even though at the time I was a long way off from having children; it changes you, forever.

The vulnerability creates connection, which creates empathy in your shared experience. It's beautiful, and simple, and synergistic.

I am so grateful to have gotten to participate and believe it has created a perspective that has balanced me and benefited me in all areas of my life.

My advice is to travel often, get into new situations, and see all of the beauty that unfolds!

Chapter 7

Memories from Morocco
from a High School Student
By Jainam Giamo

JAINAM STARTED A MICROLENDING CLUB WITH HIS HIGH SCHOOL

This guest blog comes to us from Jainam Giamo, a student at Amador Valley High School in Pleasanton, California. Since his trip to Morocco in 2016, he has started a microlending club at his high school. They had 12 members and growing as of the writing of this post!

"It's not very hot today, only 110 degrees" said the shopkeeper in Ouarzazate, Morocco. "Last week it was really hot though." Although I just finished my junior year in high school, for years now I've been intrigued by the ideas of microlending and entrepreneurship. I'm especially grateful to Olivia Hayden and Brian Doe at Whole Planet Foundation for allowing me the amazing opportunity to visit with & interview their microlending partner INMAA in Morocco, and with the many microloan recipients at the La Kasbah carpet weaving woman's cooperative in this remote oasis town in eastern Morocco.

JAINAM WITH OUR PARTNERS AT INMAA, INCLUDING SAMIRA (FAR RIGHT), WHO RECEIVED HONORABLE MENTION IN THE 2016 WPF FIELD OFFICER AWARDS

During my sophomore year in high school I joined a global business and entrepreneurship training organization called DECA which happened to have a branch at my school. I continued in DECA through my junior and now into my senior year (they made me their CFO!). Last June I wanted to find an interesting summer job, but as it turns out, it's remarkably hard to find an office job when you're still in high school and have no experience, well...really at anything! Maybe it helped that I was willing to work for free – but I was accepted into the internship program at a microlending firm in San Francisco called Kiva. I learned a lot about technology, marketing & microlending, but I yearned to get out into the field and see how these loans ACTUALLY worked and how they impacted real families.

That was when I discovered Whole Planet Foundation. They were extremely supportive of my passion, and introduced me to their lending partners at INMAA in Morocco (who were equally enthusiastic).

INMAA offered not only to meet with me, but also to tell me about microlending and to take me to meet some actual microloan recipients. I was ecstatic!

I arrived in Morocco some weeks later, and after two nights in a youth hostel in the fun but chaotic city of Marrakech, my Whole Planet adventure began.

We drove for five hours through barren moon-like landscapes interrupted occasionally by lush desert oases, and by towns clinging desperately to the main road for (economic) survival. I finally arrived (20 minutes late) at the desert town of Ouarzazate to find the INMAA staff already waiting for me in the hotel lobby.

"Way to make a great first impression," I told myself! They were so gracious, and probably more than a little curious to meet the teenager who traveled from the other side of the world to the outskirts of the Sahara Desert to meet with them—in August no less!

VISITING LA KASBAH, A WOMEN'S CARPET WEAVING COOPERATIVE. MILODA IS
A WEAVER & CLIENT OF INMAA

We talked for hours about the microlending process:
their selection criteria, the importance of the educational
component of lending, how the repayment process works
in a cash-based environment, what borrowers do with
the money, and the challenges unique to that area. Later
that day we visited the INMAA regional office as well. I
learned a lot, and I am very grateful that they took the
time to meet with me. The next day we visited La Kasbah,

a woman's carpet weaving cooperative whose members had taken many loans from INMAA (all repaid). They used the loans mainly to finance the purchase of material to make the carpets.

"This is why I came," I said to myself. It was amazingly inspiring to see & experience personally, how Whole Planet Foundation-sourced microloans have given these women not just hope, but the ability to keep an ancient tradition alive while supporting themselves and their families. I am so grateful to both the INMAA staff and Whole Planet Foundation for giving me this incredible opportunity, and for the life-changing work that they do.

Chapter 8

Rwanda, Inc. Reviewed
by Magatte Wade

By Magatte Wade

SENEGALESE ENTREPRENEUR MAGATTE WADE IS A WORLD ECONOMIC
FORUM YOUNG GLOBAL LEADER

Meet Senegalese entrepreneur Magatte Wade, friend to
Whole Planet Foundation and one of the main
contributors to the film Poverty, Inc., which examines the

darker side of the charity industry. Magatte is one of a new community of Africans who take issue with how their continent and culture are portrayed by politicians, the press, and even NGOs. From their perspective, many nonprofit initiatives fund development projects in Africa that ultimately do more harm than good. Learn more about Magatte's worldview below, where we've shared her review of the new book, Rwanda, Inc.

Rwanda, Inc: An unlikely growth story

When people think of Rwanda, they still think "genocide." Rwanda, Inc. urges them to update those thoughts. According to the authoritative Fraser Institute, which tracks an index of economic freedom for each of 144 nations, Rwanda's overall index has been one of the fastest growing in the world since the genocide. This African nation of 11 million now ranks 45th in economic freedom, higher than France, Poland, and Israel.

Journalist Patricia Crisafulli and consultant Andrea Redmond don't cite the Fraser Institute index. But they do vividly describe the transformation that has occurred in Rwanda. While economic data for developing nations are only approximations, data cited by the authors indicate just what you'd expect when economic freedom achieves a great leap forward: Rwanda has enjoyed strong economic growth accompanied by a noticeable decline in poverty.

The turnaround is largely due to the nation's current president, Paul Kagame, an extraordinary person, even in the eyes of his detractors. Growing up as a Tutsi exile in Uganda, Kagame returned to Rwanda by the early 1990s to lead an army that tried to prevent the persecution of Tutsis that had been taking place since independence in 1962. When Hutu extremists began the massacre in April 1994, U.N. troops stood by and watched it happen, along with the rest of the world. Kagame's troops swept in to stop the genocide, succeeding by July 1994, but only after more than a million people had been killed. From 1994 to 2000, a Hutu leader supported by Kagame was president. Since 2000, it has been Kagame.

Having established himself as an effective military leader, Kagame now appears to be just as effective in lifting the living standards of his people. He is also known for reducing corruption. In 2005, when Transparency International first ranked Rwanda according to its Corruption Perceptions Index, the country was 83rd. By 2011, it had moved up to 49th, making it one of the least-corrupt countries in Africa, and just ahead of Costa Rica. He also proved to be an astute investor. On the advice of Clet Niyikiza, a Rwandan Ph.D. who had been vice president of medicine development for GlaxoSmithKline, Kagame invested $16 million of Rwandan pension funds in Merrimack Pharmaceuticals, a start-up alleged to have a blockbuster cancer drug.

The authors respond to criticisms of Kagame, but not in sufficient depth to address the concerns of his detractors. One concern is that he has not permitted freedom of the press. The response of the Kagame administration is that, since the genocide, it has been necessary to limit speech that is potentially inflammatory. Crisafulli and Redmond point out that, to this day, Germany and other European nations have crimes against hate speech that are similar to the limitations imposed in Rwanda.

One indication that Kagame does not quite fit the usual dictator profile: He engaged in a public debate in front of 70,000 Twitter followers with a foreign journalist who accused him of being "despotic and deluded." Kagame is consciously modeling Rwandan reforms on those of Singapore, rated second in the world for economic freedom, but with an admittedly authoritarian government. Kagame has vowed to step down in 2017, although critics question whether he will. We have just four years to wait to see if he keeps his word.

Compared with the embarrassing parade of leaders in Africa since independence, Rwandan President Paul Kagame is clearly intelligent, disciplined, and principled. It is inspiring to read about the economic gains he has brought to the long-suffering people of Rwanda. In light of Kagame's unquestionable achievements, it would have been even more satisfying if Rwanda, Inc. had either shown us Kagame warts and all or definitively exonerated him from the most damaging charges against him. Instead, we are left to wonder: Is Kagame great only with respect to economics? Or might he be a truly great African leader?

Senegalese entrepreneur Magatte Wade is a World Economic Forum Young Global Leader. She blogs at Magatte.wordpress.com.

Chapter 9

Say All the Cornball Stuff
By Craig Jones

This guest blog comes from Craig Jones, a Team Trainer from Whole Foods Market in Andover, Massachussetts.

If you shop at any Whole Foods Market store during these first two weeks of March, in all likelihood you're going to be asked if you'd like to donate to something called the Whole Planet Foundation. Full disclosure, I work for Whole Foods and I will be doing some of the asking.

Whole Planet Foundation provides microloans all over the world to people who are attempting to start a business and lift themselves out of poverty, feed their families and chart a future course. Here are few stats:

The average first loan is $179, 88% of the recipients are women, the payback rate is 96%, 100% of donations go directly to loan recipients.

Whole Planet Foundation started in 2005, after Whole Foods Market's CEO John Mackey met Muhammad Yunus at an entrepreneurship conference. You may remember that Dr. Yunus won the 2006 Nobel Peace Prize for creating Grameen Bank as a way to provide these small (micro) loans to the world's poor. The announcement said "Lasting peace cannot be achieved unless large population groups find ways in which to break out of poverty. Micro-credit is one such means."

It may be true that the "not today" or "no, thanks" or "I'm all set" comments are a higher percentage of register transactions, but plenty of people are saying yes to adding a dollar or even five or ten (or rounding up their purchase!). We only have a few seconds with each customer, so there isn't always time for me to go into detail about how the foundation has existed since 2005, or how 100% of donations go directly to the mission of empowering women to start their own businesses.

Anyway, mid-afternoon, a woman came through my register and said yes, sure she'd throw in a dollar, and what's it all about anyway? When I explained what the foundation was, she exclaimed, "Wow that's really cool!"

I replied, "You know, $179 can change someone's life, and you don't see a 96% repayment rate even in the United States." I was thinking about how a bad day for most of us is having to deal with snow shoveling or having to delay that weekend trip to the Cape or running out of ice cream in the fridge. Some might drop $179 on a single dinner.

As I was speaking, I could feel myself getting emotional, on the verge of tears. When the customer left, I had to quickly compose myself because there were more customers. I felt deeply grateful that I work for a company that could do something that moves me enough to make me nearly cry during the work day.

It's hard to ask people that one more question, after saying thanks for spending your money here at Whole Foods today. "Would you like to spend a little more on something, the results of which you will never see?"

This isn't meant to be a paean to Whole Foods Market. I'm just taking a moment to express personal gratitude that the place I draw my paycheck and my benefits also has plenty to be proud of. See, that's the thing about gratitude. There's writing about it, maybe in a more abstract way, and there's genuinely feeling it. Most likely, just underneath where you're looking, something can be found to be grateful for, if you just look hard enough, if you look with the searching eyes of gratitude.

A fellow Team Member said of Whole Planet Foundation, "This is almost too corny to say, but we're not just selling groceries, we're selling dreams." Yes, I said, yes, say the cornball stuff! Yes, yes, I'm grateful, yes, thanks for another day of life never promised to me, yes, yes, and yes to all of it.

Chapter 10

The Spark of Entrepreneurship
By Sophie Eckrich

OUR GROUP VISITING ANOTHER GROUP OF WOMEN BORROWERS IN THE
COMMUNITY OF PATZUN

This guest blog series comes to us from Sophie Eckrich, a former Whole Planet Foundation intern and founder of Teysha.

Ten years ago, I embarked for a life-changing journey as an intern for Whole Planet Foundation with their microfinance partner, Grameen Bank, in Panajachel,

Guatemala. I was 19 years old, a rising Sophomore at the University of Texas at Austin, and I had no idea what to expect. I came away completely inspired by the spark of entrepreneurship created by microfinance and found in each woman I met in Guatemala, which has led to a very interesting and crazy past 10 years as I have started my own ethical fashion business, Teysha.

MYSELF, PHILIP SANSONE, EXECUTIVE DIRECTOR OF WHOLE PLANET FOUNDATION, AND CHIARA ATTENDING A BORROWERS MEETING IN THE CHICHICANSTENANGO REGION OF GUATEMALA.

Before going to Guatemala, I had spent time in rural Costa Rica and Ecuador, working for different NGOs on environmental projects. While traveling there, I met so many people who would tell me all the time that their greatest dream was to go to the USA to work. I looked around and saw the natural richness that they had: fertile land and family nearby. But, the opportunities to achieve more seemed few and far between. When I first heard of the concept of microfinance, it appeared to me the perfect solution for those who live in areas that do have resources nearby to be able to make something of those resources.

My long-time friend and fellow intern, Chiara, and I worked side by side with a multicultural team of Guatemalan and Bangladeshi representatives from Grameen Trust. The Guatemalan branch, Grameen Banrural, was only about one year old at the time, and the team wasted no time in bringing their lending services to some of the most remote areas of Guatemala. By the first year, they had thousands of women microfinance clients who each started with a loan of around $110 USD.

WITH THEN-DIRECTOR OF GRAMEEN BANRURAL, ALOMGIR HOSSAIN

One of the most inspiring concepts of the Grameen model of microfinance is that of "borrowers' groups," who provide the social capital to guarantee the loan. Similar to many countries in Latin America, official property rights in Guatemala can be convoluted or non-existent, which is one huge barrier to accessing a traditional bank loan. The bank has nothing to guarantee the loan, and thus the person is not eligible to receive funding.

Microfinance programs innovated to solve this issue by realizing that while the women may not have traditional property rights, they had incredibly strong social ties in their community. Thus, in order to receive a loan, a woman has to create or join a network of 6-8 other women who thereby guarantee each other's capital. You better believe if your neighbor doesn't show up to the loan meeting for whatever reason, and that affects your ability to get a loan, that you will be the first one knocking at her door to figure out what happened and to make sure she gets back on track. This system creates mutual accountability, community, as well as a group of women who are all working to create opportunities for themselves.

That summer, we traveled throughout Guatemala visiting branches and interviewing women who had received microloans. Some women used it to start a business, such as buying livestock, and others used it to expand their existing business, such as a small convenience store or a weaving business. The women most likely did not have any formal business training, but as Muhammad Yunus, the founder of Grameen Bank, wisely said, "poor people are the world's greatest entrepreneurs. Every day they have to innovate in order to survive." I witnessed firsthand the grit, resilience, and inspiration the microfinance clients possessed as they worked to create a better life for themselves and rise out of the situation in which they were born. The average microcredit client supported by WPF receives a loan of around $110 USD, depending on the country, and is then eligible for increasing amounts once she has repaid the loan.

After my experience in Guatemala, I couldn't get enough of the microfinance concept, so I went the following summer with another WPF client, Pro Mujer, in Peru. Pro Mujer operates on a similar model as the Grameen Bank, but adds in additional social service offerings such as child care, life insurance, and mobile health clinics to further support the needs of women entrepreneurs.

At the University of Texas, I ended up studying Sociology, with a minor in Latin American Studies and a certificate in International Development. The experience in the classroom would not have been the same without seeing, before my eyes, the process of poverty alleviation and both the complications and opportunities in the international development field. Through this experience, I learned that oftentimes, poverty alleviation is a multi-generational process. It starts with one woman, one mother, one person, who is able to incrementally better her circumstances and pass better opportunities on to her children. Those children, in turn, rise incrementally more. Everyone along the way works hard to strive for more than what they had, which is not unlike the history of most developed countries.

As I was nearing my graduation, the images and the stories of the microfinance entrepreneurs I had met in Guatemala and in Peru kept coming in to my mind. I knew that they had so many talents, so much potential, and were willing to work hard to achieve their dreams. They did not want a hand-out, they wanted an opportunity to work. I also knew that I possessed a similar entrepreneurial drive, and we could band together to create opportunities for the region. The seeds of my business, Teysha, were planted during those experiences and the inspiration tied together my Mexican heritage, my experiences with the Whole Planet Foundation, and my studies at UT. The idea of using fashion as a medium for empowerment came naturally after seeing the vast quantities of incredible textiles and artisans in Guatemala, Peru, and beyond.

Teysha: The Beginnings

After graduating from the University of Texas, I knew that I wanted to work in Latin America, do something that improved the lives of others, and do something that was interesting to me. I looked at jobs in the International Development field, however, most of them at that time required a graduate degree and multiple years of experience. Being the impatient person that I am, I was ready to get started on working on my dream career path, on my own terms. I figured I didn't have much to lose to at least try and start my own project.

I thought back to the women artisans I had met in Guatemala and Peru, tons of women with *incredible*, handwoven textiles and pieces of art, who were literally standing on the side of the road in a remote area, trying to sell their textiles. I knew that those textiles possessed incredible cultural significance and woven histories. I also knew that as they were, the textiles in themselves were a bit unapproachable to the modern "consumer" since people had remarked there were only so many ways to display a textile. It was clear to me that the textiles, if they were to create more opportunities for the artisans, needed to find another way for people to connect to them. My goal was to create as many opportunities for the artisans as possible and to do that, the textiles needed to approachable and create value for someone.

A WOMAN FROM SANTA CATARINA LA LAGUNA, GUATEMALA, WEAVING ON A TRADITIONAL BACKSTRAP LOOM. IT'S AN INCREDIBLY INTRICATE PROCESS!

The idea of shoes came as something that was useful in everyday life, and as it happened, was also a traditional craft that employed people in rural Latin America. As any person with a modicum of retail experience will tell you, shoes are *the most difficult* thing to do, the inventory, the sizing, the fit, oh my goodness... Luckily, I had zero retail experience, and not much business experience, so the idea sounded like a grand adventure. And thus, the idea for Teysha was ready to launch — creating artisan made goods with a modern and functional design.

TWO YOUNG GIRLS HELPING THEIR MOTHER SELL TEXTILES AROUND LAKE ATITLAN, GUATEMALA. WHILE THE TEXTILES ARE SO BEAUTIFUL, SOMETIMES THEY NEED TO BE PRESENTED IN A WAY THAT IS MORE APPROACHABLE TO SOMEONE. MY GOAL IS TO PROVIDE AS MUCH WORK FOR THE WOMEN AS POSSIBLE, SO THEY ARE LESS RELIANT ON DAILY SALES.

After traveling through several countries in Latin America looking for artisan shoemakers, I remembered having visited a small town in Guatemala in 2008 during my Whole Planet Foundation internship where you could have custom-made cowboy boots within a few days. It seemed like the perfect place to centralize Teysha's operations due to the plethora of textile artisans, leather artisans, and just the creative energy in general.

As a startup, my team and I did not have the capital to invest in making a bunch of shoes, thus came the idea of custom-made boots. Choose your textile, leather, and shoe style, and we will make it for you! It was a crazy idea, but it turned out to be our secret sauce for getting started.

MUCH OF MY BEGINNING STAGES OF TEYSHA WERE SPENT MEETING AND
LEARNING FROM DIFFERENT ARTISANS, TRYING TO FIGURE OUT HOW I COULD
HELP BRING MARKET ACCESS

We found a small group of shoemakers in Pastores, Guatemala, who were able to make the first batch, and we started to promote the idea on our nascent Facebook page. I was stunned by the amount of traction we received initially, and it was definitely a validation for the market and that people did want cool, customizable, unique goods.

Advice for Future Entrepreneurs

For anyone who has an idea of something they'd like to try as a business, I truly believe it is so easy now to get started very simply and at least test the idea and see if there is a market for it. The worst thing, in my opinion, would be to spend months or years and tons of money investing in an idea or product without getting feedback

341

or finding your target market, only to find after launch that there actually wasn't a need for your good or service.

A PHOTO OF THE FIRST BATCH OF CUSTOM BOOTS TEYSHA CREATED IN GUATEMALA – ONE OF A KIND AND FEATURING HAND-WOVEN AND UPCYCLED TEXTILES.

The great thing about starting from little to no experience is that you are learning every single day, trying new things, and basically realizing that there is no right or wrong way to do things. The first few years were full of different in-person events, pop-up-shops, figuring out how to market and sell online, trying wholesale relationships, making new products, and building out our supply chain and production team. Throughout the whole experience, the team from Whole Planet Foundation has provided incredible guidance on both the impact and business side, and really cheered Teysha on every step of the way.

ONE OF MY FAVORITE PARTS OF GROWING THE BUSINESS HAS BEEN MEETING ARTISANS THROUGHOUT GUATEMALA AND LEARNING MORE ABOUT THEIR NEEDS, ABILITIES, AND DREAMS.

Today, six years after incorporating, Teysha works with 15 shoemakers in Pastores, Guatemala, we have a robust network of women artisans and small-businesses who we work with to create textiles, and we have an ever-expanding collection of shoes and accessories. Every day is different, and I am always kept on my toes by the growth of our social enterprise.

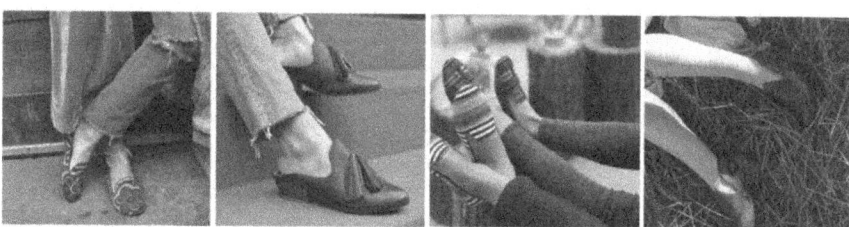

TEYSHA HAS GROWN TO HAVE AN AMAZING ARRAY OF HANDCRAFTED SHOES AND ACCESSORIES – I AM CONTINUOUSLY IMPRESSED BY THE CREATIVITY OF OUR TEAM AND ARTISANS

Part IX
FIELD OFFICER APPRECIATION

Chapter 1

Field Officers in Microfinance
By Stephanie Manciagli

"Microfinance has always been a high-touch business, with personal contact playing an indispensable role in the delivery of financial services for low-income clients. Human relationships and values like trust and empathy are crucial in determining whether a microfinance institution (MFI) will be able to grow and remain sustainable. And it is the MFIs' frontline staff – the loan officers and other field staff – who must uphold these values and relationships with their clients, presenting the face of the MFI to their most important public – their clients." (quoted from Want to Stay in Business? Keep your Loan Officers Happy).

Microfinance institutions' frontline workers have many names, like Field Officers, Loan Officer, Credit Agents, Portfolio Managers, Facilitators and Advisors. We call them Field Officers. These Field Officers become the face of their institutions, as they often take on many roles with clients: assessing potential clients, allotting credit to selected clients, convening bi-weekly group meetings, and engaging clients in dynamic trainings.

For many Field Officers, the job doesn't stop there. Unlike at traditional banks, Field Officers for microfinance institutions need to travel daily to villages and often to the homes of their clients as a key part of building a bond with the entrepreneurs they want to ensure succeed with the loans they take. This means long days spent in different communities, unexpected dangers or obstacles and putting in overtime to help a client that may need some extra mentorship or support to succeed.

In July 2014, Whole Planet Foundation piloted a new Field Officer Appreciation Award in the Africa/MENA region. We asked all of our Africa/MENA partners to internally nominate their strongest field officer and submit her or his story to WPF for consideration in the competition. After being nominated by their institution, WPF's large network votes for the most remarkable nominees and then, the top 5 finalists are recognized with awards and each finalist receives a $500 prize. Hearing the personal accomplishments and stories of hope inspired us to offer the award in each region where we work, to show appreciation to these frontline warriors.

While WPF partners with organizations across distinct socio-geographic and political landscapes, we've found over the years that the best Field Officers share several traits in common: dedication, creativity, inclusiveness and leadership.

Dedication

Field Officers often travel great distances on bad roads to reach clients in rural areas who may be tens of kilometers from each other. To keep costs low, they go by public transportation, on foot, or on a motorbike. On top of all that travel, they also have to complete desk work to keep their records up to date. Past winners of the Field Officer Appreciation Award, like Ramboa, regularly arrive at the office by 5:00 a.m., start visiting clients at 6:00

a.m., and sometimes stay at the office into the night, until 9:00 p.m.

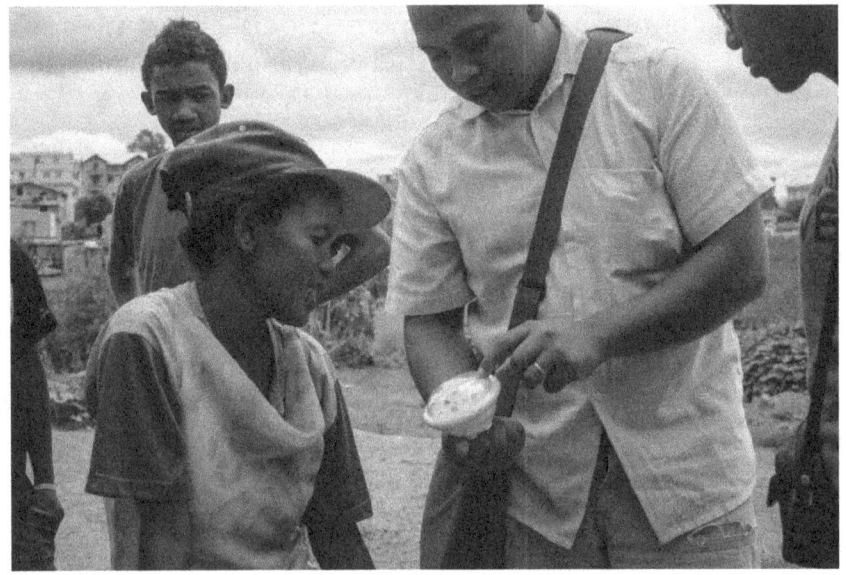

RAMBOA FROM WPF MADAGASCAR PARTNER JIRO-VE SHOWS A MICROCREDIT CLIENT HOW TO OPERATE A SOLAR LAMP.

Creativity

Microfinance clients often have little financial cushion and are especially vulnerable to shocks related to illness and death, unpredictable climate, and market volatility. Many of WPF's partners have nominated colleagues who use creativity and flexibility to help clients navigate financial difficulties and start or expand their businesses. One Field Officer nominee used his time to proactively connect his clients to outside opportunities, and even helped a client win a youth microfinance prize which came with an award to support the growth of the business. Another Field Officer worked closely with a client who faced emotional and financial setbacks from two family deaths; the client has now grown her business and graduated from a very small group loan to a larger individual loan.

Inclusiveness

Many of the winners were especially committed to the financial inclusion of disenfranchised communities. Winners included field officers who dedicate extra effort in outreach to youth, women, people with disabilities, and people with HIV positive status.

FABRICE, FROM TOGO: A SECOND-TIER WINNER IN THE 2019 AWARDS, PICTURED WITH MICROCREDIT CLIENTS ON AFRICAN WOMEN'S DAY.

Leadership

Our partners also highlighted each Field Officer's contributions to organizational growth. Many of the winners helped open new branches and areas, execute innovations, represent their organizations in external partnerships, and help mentor and train colleagues.

Chapter 2

Field Officers in Microfinance: Unbelievable Stories from our Partners
By Stephanie Manciagli

It's almost hard to believe what Field Officers are capable of and hearing their stories has provided constant motivation for our team. Here are some of their stories:

Paul, GHAPE

Paul, a Field Officer from GHAPE, in Cameroon, has risen above the odds to provide service to microcredit clients in his community. Here is what GHAPE had to say about Paul's unrelenting determination to continue serving loan groups, despite the risk to his own safety during an ongoing civil conflict in the country:

"During the current civil war in Northwest Cameroon, Paul has experienced the worst of it at his branch and presently, the movement of bikes and cars around his working area have been banned. In one of the group meetings, he was taken by the secessionist group and was physically attacked as the group thought he was working with the Government. Thanks to the cooperation of members, alarm was raised and members of that women's center and other women's centers in the community quickly rushed there for his rescue and to testify he is working with an NGO. He vows not to stop serving his members even as he is trekking for hours to meet them in their different localities."

Marceline, Thrive Zimbabwe

MARCELINE WITH A GROUP OF HER BORROWERS

Marceline, a Field Officer at Thrive Zimbabwe, shared a story which demonstrates the unpredictability of Thrive's work:

"Most of the group members [live] spaced out and also coming from far places. I recall one time I had to walk 20 kilometers from a [women's group] Centre to the point where I would get transport and it was dark already. Many thanks to the lorry driver who was carrying vegetables to the market as he was kind to give me a lift only to get home at midnight. At one point in time, I went for site visits with two colleagues. I traveled on foot to assess two women's groups whom had told me their houses were near the shops, only to discover that was not the case. I finished late and ended up being accompanied back by a borrower's son on a donkey driven scotch cart. It was a moment of laughter when my colleagues saw me in the cart."

Mr. Islam, SUPPORT

Mr. Islam, a Field Officer for SUPPORT in Bangladesh, had a very difficult livelihood. His father passed away when he was 8 and so he had to struggle very much to

350

afford education and care for his family. He finished his education by working during his studies but never lost hope of being a good human being. He is one of the most hardworking employees of SUPPORT, and despite his daily transportation hurdles to meet clients, he successfully completes his duties.

SUPPORT shares that, "In July 2019, a severe flood hit the char areas, primarily those covered under the Rowmari branch. In such a situation, the only mode of transport across the areas is using a banana boat. Mr. Rafijul did not stop his work but rather with sheer dedication, he continued to visit the SUPPORT clients. However, one day during such a visit, Rafijul's banana boat had turned upside down in the water. Thankfully he had swam across flooded zone to a highlight but the most astonishing part was that during the entire swim, he tried to protect his client's documents by keeping them up in the air."

Keren, Grameen Costa Rica

Grameen Costa Rica shared, in one nomination, that the evolution of Field Officer Keren Cruz's quality of work, for and with her clients, has been outstanding.

"She has been the Officer with the largest intake of new clients in the organization. Keren has been able to bring in up to 64 new clients in a single month and has a monthly average of 36. She is proactive, dynamic, and committed, to the extent that group members themselves express satisfaction feeling they are with an organization which gives them the opportunity to get ahead and empowers them to achieve what they set out to do.

Qualitatively, Keren (center, in the photo above) is an officer who has the necessary tools to convey confidence and discipline. Clients tell us that for them, Keren's service is more than just a loan, it is accompaniment, empathy, respect, understanding, and support. They truly feel the love she has for them through her work. She is always developing motivational topics that inject positivity into group meetings."

Uribiades, Microserfin

Uribiades, who works for Microserfin in Panamá, is fiercely committed to the improvement of his clients' quality of life. Microserfin shared that "He is dedicated and honest, always going the extra mile. Since he began to work as a Loan Officer in the Darien province, Uribiades has been able to improve his own life, mainly by securing his family's livelihood obtaining credit at banks and buying a motorcycle which helps in his field work (he frequently goes to areas that can only be accessed on foot, horseback, or motorcycle).

 Uribiades recalls a time during the rainy season, when he was out in the field for a client credit assessment. Trying to take a shortcut, he got lost for three hours in the mountainous area, finally finding his way out guiding himself with the sun. He found the client's home, somehow arriving from the rear side of the property. On his way back after the visit, it began to rain heavily, and the creeks and rivers rose so much that he could not get out for yet another three hours. He was soaking wet and muddy, but happy to have completed the job!

Microserfin nominated Uribiades due to his effective portfolio management, his strong client relationships, and his commitment to the organization.

Gloria, Friendship Bridge

Gloria is Friendship Bridge's (FB's) longest serving Facilitator, having started in 2003. As of 2019, she had a client portfolio of over 580 women who she supports with education and microcredit. Gloria's work, problem-resolution, and strong communication skills are widely recognized across Sololá, Guatemala where she works.

Gloria is the youngest of eight children, from a farming family. She started helping at age eight with the coffee harvest. Thanks to her father's belief in hard work and education, five out of the eight siblings finished high school.

About Friendship Bridge's vision and mission, Gloria says, "I was struck by Friendship Bridge's support of women through credit and non-formal education." She has two daughters and a son, so the focus on women's education is important to her.

Ms. Nguyen Thi Du, Mekong Plus Vietnam

Ms. Du was nominated by Mekong Plus Vietnam for her work mobilizing community resources to provide scholarships for borrowers' children and donations for borrowers with chronic illnesses.

MS. NGUYEN THI DU (LEFT) WITH A CLIENT.

Mekong Plus split the award between a bonus for Ms. Du, purchasing tools for a program teaching children with disabilities; contribution towards the medical treatment of a sick member of one of the participants and lastly to purchase a motorbike for a participating household!

Conclusions

These accounts highlight the dedication, technical expertise and strong client relationships that Field

Officers bring to make the microfinance institutions they work for a success. While on paper, we know that their job is to support micro-entrepreneurs to make sound investment decisions to grow their small business activities, it is evident that so many go above and beyond this role. Thank you to all field officers for offering your hard work and dedication to clients, over the years. You are truly agents of change.

Part X
FUNDING WHOLE PLANET FOUNDATION

Chapter 1

The Stakeholder Model
By Joy Stoddard

UNILEVER'S JOHN FITZGERALD (CENTER) WITH STAFF, LEADERSHIP, AND FIELD CREDIT OFFICERS OF SMALL ENTERPRISE FOUNDATION, WHOLE PLANET FOUNDATION'S MICROFINANCE PARTNER IN SOUTH AFRICA.

"Through the Whole Planet Foundation, we want to help end poverty around the world by making microcredit working-capital loans to millions of impoverished people to

help them create and improve their businesses" - John Mackey, CEO and Co-Founder, Whole Foods Market

Created in 2005, Whole Planet Foundation's collaborative approach to fundraising is inspired by Whole Foods Market's dynamic stakeholder model. This approach toward the people who have an interest or an investment in what the company does or sells, including shoppers, employees (called team members), suppliers, corporate partners and our parent company Amazon is a unique form of conscious capitalism. Sourcing coffee, tea, tropical fruit and vegetables, spices, cacao and more from a place means that Whole Foods Market and its stakeholders feel an obligation to give back, in this case to support the people living in poverty in communities around the world that supply stores with products. John Mackey had the vision in 2004 to launch Whole Planet Foundation to help a million people, and through June 2020 it has funded more than 22 million opportunities for people to change their own lives through entrepreneurship.

Because the Foundation's operating costs are covered by Whole Foods Market, donors can give with confidence that 100 percent of donations benefit microcredit clients. Whole Planet Foundation's first donors were Whole Foods Market shoppers through a company-wide Community 5% Day on October 25, 2005, where the company donated five percent of after-tax profits - $525,000 - to seed the foundation. In 2006, Whole Planet Foundation launched an Annual Prosperity Campaign that has raised shopper support of $46 million in donations through the registers. In 2007, many Whole Foods Market employees became donors by signing up to contribute $1 per paycheck, and now Team Member

Giving through payroll deduction has surpassed $10 million for microcredit. In John Mackey's book, Conscious Capitalism, he states on page 131: "Probably nothing we have done in our history at Whole Foods Market has raised the morale of the organization more than the work of this foundation; our team members are so excited and proud of what we're doing to help end poverty."

Going further in 2007, Whole Planet Foundation launched giving levels for suppliers to engage in our mission. Suppliers to Whole Foods Market donate via scanbacks, small contributions like one percent of sales or five cents per item, up to the Ten Thousand Dollar Fund, the Poverty Is Unnecessary Fund at $25,000, the Supplier Alliance for Microcredit at $50,000 and most recently through the $100,000 Fund. In 2014, Papyrus-Recycled Paper Greetings showed up to our headquarters office with literally a big check! They donated $100,000 to Whole Planet Foundation that day, so we launched the $100,000 Fund in their honor. Thanks to their initial generosity, this fund has raised more than $2.4 million to date and suppliers have contributed more than $14 million to date to alleviate poverty through Whole Planet Foundation.

From 2008-2019, Whole Foods Market's Whole Tradc program donated one percent of sales, $21 million, to Whole Planet Foundation, corporate partners like Amazon, Chase Bank and car2go have surpassed $2.6 million, online donors have surpassed $1 million, individual donors have contributed over half a million dollars and events like Whole Planet Foundation's Annual Party with a Purpose have raised a quarter of a million dollars. These varied fundraising platforms enable our stakeholders to join our mission in a turn-key way, in the manner that is most successful and strategic for them. Whole Planet Foundation is proud of our Platinum Transparency Rating on Charity Navigator, the highest level of non-profit recognition.

To further engage our donors and advocates, we host them in the field to witness the transformative power of microcredit. The Whole Foods Market Team Member Volunteer Program provides a life-changing experience for team members to see microcredit in action and provide service in countries where Whole Planet Foundation alleviates poverty, and in participating they become our greatest ambassadors. Thanks to the success of this program, we started inviting suppliers to join Whole Planet Foundation for impact visits, hosting more than 250 donors since 2010 in Costa Rica, Guatemala, Brazil, Paraguay, Togo, South Africa, India, Thailand and in a dozen cities in the United States. Domestic visits to Harlem, New York, Miami, Florida, Oakland, California and Austin, Texas are detailed in this book's United States section.

The aim of the international impact visits is to understand the root causes of poverty that create dire conditions in countries and also to understand the culture, language, food, traditions and destinations that make the country so rich, so to speak, so that they can see what is possible for people living in poverty to attain. Everyone has the right to flourish!

2010 International Impact Visit to Peru

We landed in Lima, tried traditional food such as purple potatoes and quinoa smoothies, visited Arequipa where Whole Foods Market was sourcing onions, partnered with Fly the Phoenix to learn about water tanks for marginalized families in that area, transited to Puno to spend time with our microfinance partner Pro Mjuer, and finally, we visited mystical Machu Picchu. There were 13 suppliers and Whole Foods Market Team Members on this trip!

MICROCREDIT CLIENTS WITH SRETEN GAIJIC OF CASCAL, A COCA-COLA BRAND. OTHER SUPPLIER DONORS INCLUDED JOE BROWNE OF SEVENTH GENERATION AND JILL GRIFFITH FROM IZZE AND NAKED JUICE.

Pro Mujer offers low-income women the means to transform their lives and those of their loved ones through financial services, empowerment and business training, and health services. Our visit included seeing a health clinic operate within the microfinance branch and understanding the importance of mobile medical units to conduct pap smear tests in the field where microcredit clients could take advantage of this convenient, affordable service designed to reduce the rate of cervical cancer in the area.

2011 International Impact Visit to India

We landed for an overnight in Mumbai, the second most populous city and the capital city of the Indian state of Maharashtra, and took in the contrasts of life that India offers. We then hopped a regional flight to Thiruvananthapuram, the capital of the Indian State of Kerala. Located on the west coast of India near the extreme south of the mainland, this city has 1,000,000 inhabitants and is the largest and most populous city in Kerala. There we met with Microcredit Initiative of Grameen in Kerala, where the local Director Golok Chandra Roy taught us about clients like Vanaja.

WHOLE FOODS MARKET TEAM MEMBER DOROTHY, PAYAL MALHOTRA FROM CAFÉ SPICE, MICROCREDIT CLIENT VANAJA AND GENÈVE STEWART OF CASCAL

Vanaja took a loan to purchase threads and other items needed for weaving traditional saris of Kerala, and a subsequent loan to buy a loom. A few women told us they used to work for hours in a local sari factory employing their talents with no way to save any of their paltry income. Now, women like Vanaja can even rent out their loom to other women weavers in the community, providing a win-win opportunity for both parties. Their talent, speed and efficiency in weaving was impressive and the finished products simply gorgeous.

MIG-Kerala intended to expand access to credit to 4,500 women in this part of India where Whole Foods Market sources a variety of products including cashews, so we enjoyed a visit to a cashew farm where we learned not to gobble them up as their harvest and sorting is a formidable, respectable task! Then we transited north to Delhi and visited the Taj Mahal.

2012 International Impact Visit to Brazil

After landing in Sao Paolo, the capital city of Brazil with 12 million inhabitants and the 10th richest city in the world at the time of our visit, we met with Whole Planet Foundation microfinance partner Banco do Povo.

We learned about their operations at their modest office and moved around the city visiting microcredit clients at their places of business. We capped off the experience at Iguazu Falls, where the Brazilian and Argentine falls together make up the largest waterfall in the world.

OUR GROUP OF DONORS LEARNING FROM BANCO DO POVO AT THEIR HEADQUARTERS OFFICE: VALERIE BROWN AND VICTORIA NUEVO-CELESTE FROM STACY'S AND NAKED JUICE, SUSAN JOHNSON FROM SEVENTH GENERATION, KEN BLAKEMAN AND ROSALI MIDDLEMAN FROM GENJI, RON BLITZER FROM BE GREEN PACKAGING, AND JAMES HOAGLAND FROM ITO EN AND WHOLE PLANET FOUNDATION.

Banco do Povo serves people living in poverty in urban areas near Sao Paulo where EcoPath sources cleaning products sold in Whole Foods Market, including the favelas ("slums") where Banco do Povo employs a unique model of group-based lending to clients that are considered too high risk for any other institution.

Our experience meeting clients in the favelas was inspiring as they have a network of community support there as well as regular customers, and our group felt safe and welcomed in an atmosphere of solidarity. People all over the world have similar basic needs and desires, a common linkage for us all to cherish.

2013 International Impact Visit to Thailand

Our group landed in Bangkok and visited stunning Buddhist temples, then took an overnight train to Surin where Alter Eco and its partners grow the rice it sells to Whole Foods Market, then moved up north to the Chang Mai area where Whole Planet Foundation microfinance partner Small Enterprise Development (SED) operates.

SUPPLIER DONORS SARAH MEDLIN OF SEVENTH GENERATION (CENTER BOTTOM) AND KEN BLAKEMAN WITH GENJI SUSHI (BOTTOM RIGHT) LEARNING HOW TO MAKE JEWELRY FROM MICROCREDIT CLIENTS OF SED.

SED is a microfinance institution that works with women in villages in the poorest provinces of Thailand, focusing primarily on the village banking methodology. A village bank is a community association consisting of groups of five to seven women each, together creating a larger group of thirty to eighty members who meet regularly and are provided with microcredit loans. The clients we met were artisans who could make jewelry and home goods, weave traditional Thai silks, and even start with growing the silkworms themselves, to make the most profit for their handiwork.

MICROCREDIT CLIENT MAKING SILK FOR WEAVING BY BOILING SILK WORMS

Taking a microcredit loan from SED provided opportunities to purchase items in bulk, merchandise finished products for sale villages and marketplaces, and have the support of SED staff and each other.

2015 International Impact Visit to the Togolese Republic
We landed in Lomé, the capital and largest city in Togo, a West African country of more than 7 million people, and one of the world's poorest countries. Our host was Alaffia, which is run by Togolese people, mostly women, led by CEO Olowo'n-djo Tchala and his family, and sources shea butter and coconut oil and other raw ingredients

from cooperatives of women all over Togo. Then the products are finished, packaged and sold in the United States at Whole Foods Market and other retailers. Alaffia is also a donor to Whole Planet Foundation, geo-targeting its $100,000 donation to Whole Planet Foundation's microfinance partner Entrepreneurs du Monde who serves marginalized women in Lomé, with plans to grow outside the city.

ALAFFIA CEO AND CO-FOUNDER OLOWO'N-DJO TCHALA WITH MICROCREDIT CLIENT WHO SELLS BEVERAGES IN THE LOCAL MARKETPLACE.

Our group of supplier donors included Tony Huston and Melanie Guidotti of Papyrus-Recycled Paper Greetings, Kaze Williams of Reserveage, Gayle Grindley of Seventh Generation, Olowo'n-djo Tchala and JoAnne Brenner of Alaffia and me.

We had the pleasure of staying with the Tchala family in rustic lodges in the city and further north in the Sokode area, where we volunteered at an elementary school supported by Alaffia and aided in basic construction for a day.

MELANIE GUIDOTTI OF PAPYRUS-RECYCLED PAPER GREETINGS AND KAZE WILLIAMS OF RESERVEAGE AT A MICROCREDIT CLIENT MEETING WHERE CLIENTS ARE LEARNING ABOUT USING THEIR LOAN PRINCIPAL FOR BUSINESS PURPOSES AS COMPARED TO PERSONAL EXPENSES.

Entrepreneurs du Monde created Assilassimé (which means Hand in Hand in the Ewe language) to support the most vulnerable. They offer microloans and extensive social support, working with over 30 associations which refer those living with a disability or with HIV who are then are asked to form loan groups of microentrepreneurs so that they can make progress together.

Togo is a country experiencing the problem of extreme poverty, but the opportunities provided by Assilassimé and Alaffia showed two strong organizations determined to work side by side with working people to uplift communities.

2016 International Impact Visit to Guatemala

We landed in Guatemala City to visit the Mayan Museum and took a short ride to the city of Antigua, founded in the early 16th century in the central highlands of the country. After visiting preserved Spanish architecture, we departed for Mayan ruins Iximche on our way to Lake Atitlan around which Whole Planet Foundation microfinance partner Friendship Bride offers microcredit to Mayan women.

WITH FRIENDSHIP BRIDGE AND MICROCREDIT CLIENTS IN HUEHUETENANGO, GUATEMALA, AND OUR GROUP OF DONORS. PHOTO COURTESY OF HIBALL ENERGY.

According to their website, Friendship Bridge "provides microfinance, education, and preventive health services to help clients build resilience and pursue opportunities. The average Friendship Bridge client is a 37 year-old Mayan woman whose household earns between $1.11 and $4.16 a day. On average she has only 3.4 years of formal education, has four children, cannot read or write, and is unlikely to speak Spanish, the official language of Guatemala. All of this adds up to an inability to secure a loan that might better her situation."

Our group witnessed these barriers from the perspective of microfinance and opportunity. The women pictured above either run small convenience stores out of their home and/or grow potatoes and raise a few sheep as their business. If a client is just growing potatoes, however, it is a challenge to repay the loan every two weeks, until harvest. By the next growing season, Friendship Bridge had developed an agriculture loan product, designed to support a client through potato harvest. Friendship Bridge, like many of our microfinance partners, listened to their clients and improved a service for them.

A MICROCREDIT CLIENT OF FRIENDSHIP BRIDGE WITH GAYLE GRINDLEY

2018 International Impact Visit to Nepal

We landed in Kathmandu, the capital city of 1 million people, and visited Whole Planet Foundation microfinance partner Nirdhan Utthan Bank, Limited, at their headquarters office to learn about their operations before taking a regional flight to a branch in the Ilam District where Whole Foods Market was sourcing green tea. The name of the bank in Nepalese means Bank for the Upliftment of the Poor.

NIRDHAN'S LEADERSHIP STAFF INCLUDING CEO JANARDAN PANT AND OUR GROUP OF DONORS (JULIET MORAN AND JASON RAHLAN FROM CHOBANI, DAVID SUGERIK FROM PAPYRUS-RECYCLED PAPER GREETINGS, MICHELLE LONG AND HOPE FURST FROM PEPSICO NATURAL BRANDS AND KAZE WILLIAMS FROM RESERVEAGE, WHOLE PLANET FOUNDATION'S REGIONAL DIRECTOR FOR ASIA/PACIFIC CLAIRE KELLY, DIGITAL FUNDRAISING SPECIALIST OLIVIA HAYDEN AND ME.

Nirdhan provides microcredit loans, savings, microinsurance and remittances. It has a self-reliant group methodology that enables field staff to efficiently manage members across remote areas. Our group had travelled from various points in the United States to Kathmandu, Nepal and then took that flight 1.5 hour flight into the Ilam district, then a 3 hour car ride and once we met Nirdhan staff we travelled for about 30 minutes by car and then walked 15 minutes into forested land to meet with clients. Nirdhan's support enables those women to take advantage! The clients we met ranged in age from young to older and typical businesses included neighborhood kiosks that served as mini-convenience stores, trinkets and jewelry, small restaurants and tea farming. Our group even had the pleasure of eating lunch at a microcredit client restaurant after meeting women at a collection and disbursement meeting at a tea farm.

A LOAN REPAYMENT MEETING WITH WOMEN. CLIENTS SUPPORT EACH OTHER AND ARE SUPPORTED BY THE MICROFINANCE ORGANIZATION.

2019 International Impact Visit to South Africa

We landed in Johannesburg and learned about the country's history at the Apartheid Museum, before heading to the Nelspruit area where Whole Planet Foundation microfinance partner Small Enterprise Foundation supports entrepreneurs living in the Kruger

National Park area, an area of affluent visitors where people are living in poverty. Our group included PepsiCo Premium Natural (Naked Juice/KeVita) Director-Natural Channel Michelle Long, Senior Customer Manager Sara Martindale and Natural Channel Field Strategy Katie Kowalski, Stacy's Customer Management Director of Sales Lisa Honeycutt, Unilever/Seventh Generation Business Manager John Fitzgerald, Primal Kitchen Vice President of Sales-Natural Reno Yanes, Advocate Gayle Grindley, Travel Logistics Coordinator Barbara Joubert, Whole Planet Foundation's Digital Fundraising Specialist Olivia Hayden and me.

At the time of our visit, Whole Planet Foundation had disbursed $1,500,000 to Small Enterprise Foundation whose motto is "Imagine a World Free of Poverty, Where Every Woman Has the Chance to Realize Her Potential". Our support has created 124,261 microloans for 100% women entrepreneurs with an average loan size of approximately $212 and a 100% repayment rate. Our Board of Directors just approved a third project grant of $900,000 so that we can reach more people together.

We left our lodge at six thirty in the morning to meet Small Enterprise Foundation and split up in small groups to meet diverse groups of clients at different tenures and different levels of success. SEF has a policy of limiting visitors to 3 people at one time, so we were led by branch manager Moses Ngamba and with zonal managers for client comfort. It was a powerful day meeting women with no formal education but thriving microbusinesses!

Small Enterprise Foundation's motto is Imagine a World Free of Poverty. Their goal is to help every woman reach her potential through microcredit to women living in poor, rural communities. They identify clients using two assessment tools: a Poverty Probability Index (an industry-standard poverty assessment survey which indicates the likelihood that a household lives below a certain poverty line) and the Participatory Wealth Ranking (a relative definition of poverty established by stakeholders within the community). SEF employs a group-based lending methodology and a focus on a group savings program for the clients to build up and rely on in times of trouble.

WHOLE PLANET FOUNDATION'S JOY STODDARD (RIGHT) WITH MICHELLE LONG (LEFT) AND A MICROCREDIT CLIENT OF SMALL ENTERPRISE FOUNDATION IN SOUTH AFRICA.

For the last part of our trip, in order to get to meet and learn about other vulnerable populations in South Africa, we volunteered at the Steilhoogte School of 300 children and helped them construct a stage for school events under a tent outside. We then visited the Cape of Good

Hope and later departed for home, feeling better educated about solutions to poverty and how we can all work together to create sustainable solutions to eliminate it.

AFTERWORD
& Suggestions
for Future Reading

After learning more about our work to empower entrepreneurs, you may feel compelled to get involved in our mission to promote economic justice and financial inclusion. Whole Foods Market pays for our overhead expenses, so all donations go directly to the beneficiaries. Our success depends on donations from Whole Foods Market team members, suppliers, customers and from individuals and other businesses.

To support our work, you can donate any time by visiting our website, wholeplanetfoundation.org. 100% of your donation will go to a microentrepreneur, since Whole Foods Market pays for all overhead expenses for the foundation. Visit wholeplanetfoundation.org/donate to make a generous gift to our cause.

The resources below can help you learn more about the root causes of poverty, what traditional development does wrong, and why microfinance can be a sustainable solution for people living in poverty.

Microfinance:
- Banker to the Poor: Microlending and the Battle Against World Poverty, *by Muhammad Yunus*
- Poor Economics: A Radical Rethinking of the Way to Fight Global Poverty, *by Abhijit Banerjee and Ester Duflo*
- Poverty Capital: Microfinance and the Making of Development, *by Ananya Roy*

International Development:

- Poor People, *by William T. Vollmann*
- The Beautiful Tree: A Personal Journey into How the World's Poorest People are Educating Themselves, *by James Tooley*
- The Stealth of Nations: The Global Rise of the Informal Economy, *by Robert Neuwirth*
- Portfolios of the Poor: How the World's Poor Live on $2 a Day, *by Daryl Collins et al*
- The Other Path: Economic Answers to Terrorism, *by Hernando de Soto*

What Went Wrong with Traditional Development Models:

- The White Man's Burden: Why the West's Efforts to Aid the Rest Have Done So Much Ill and So Little Good, *by William Easterly*
- Dead Aid: Why Aid Is Not Working and How There Is a Better Way for Africa, *by Dambisa Moyo*
- The Bottom Billion: Why the Poorest Countries are Failing and What Can Be Done About it, *by Paul Collier*
- The Tyranny of Experts: Economists, Dictators, and the Forgotten Rights of the Poor, *by William Easterly*
- Poverty, Inc.: Fighting Poverty is Big Business, video documentary *by Michael Matheson Miller et al*
- The Idealist: Jeffrcy Sachs and the Quest to End Poverty, *by Nina Munk*

Economics and Capitalism

- Conscious Capitalism: Liberating the Historic Spirit of Business, *by John Mackey and Rajendra Sisodia*
- In Defense of Global Capitalism, *by Johan Norberg*

- Free to Choose: A Personal Statement, *by Milton and Rose Friedman*
- The Road to Serfdom, *by F.A. Hayek*
- Good Capitalism, Bad Capitalism: and the Economics of Growth and Prosperity, *by William J. Baumol et al*

Environmentalism & Its Impact on World Poverty

- Whole Earth Discipline: Why Dense Cities, Nuclear Power, Transgenic Crops, Restored Wildlands, and Geoengineering are Necessary, *by Stuart Brand*
- Confessions of a Greenpeace Dropout: The Making of a Sensible Environmentalist, *by Patrick Moore*
- Power Hungry: The Myths of Green Energy and the Real Fuels of the Future, *by Robert Bryce*
- Cool It: The Skeptical Environmentalist's Guide to Global Warming, *by Bjorn Lomborg*
- Just Food: Where Locavores Get it Wrong and How We Can Truly Eat Responsibly, *by James E. McWilliams*

A more complete list of resources can be found at: www.wholeplanetfoundation.org/get-involved/learn/